# THE COSMIC SHEKINAH

*"The first human never finished comprehending wisdom,*
*nor will the last succeed in fathoming her."*
~ Jesus Sirach 24:28, Ben Sira, C2nd BCE.

# About the Authors

**Sorita d'Este and David Rankine** have both been exploring the history of religion, magic and mysticism for as long as they can remember. They have been working together since late 2000, producing hundreds of articles for journals, magazines and part-works; facilitating workshops and lecturing on the Kabbalah, Mysticism and Magic at national and international events. Between them they have authored more than 30 published books to date, many of which are on the subject of renaissance and medieval magic, religion, mythology and folklore.

If you enjoy *The Cosmic Shekinah*, you may also enjoy the following titles by the same authors:

### Sorita d'Este & David Rankine
Hekate Liminal Rites (Avalonia, 2009)
Practical Qabalah Magick (Avalonia, 2009)
The Isles of the Many Gods (Avalonia, 2007)
Visions of the Cailleach (Avalonia, 2009)
The Guises of the Morrigan (Avalonia, 2005)

### Sorita d'Este
Artemis: Virgin Goddess of the Sun & Moon (Avalonia, 2006)
Both Sides of Heaven (anthology), Avalonia, 2009
Hekate Her Sacred Fires (anthology), (Avalonia, 2010)

### David Rankine
Climbing the Tree of Life (Avalonia, 2006)
The Book of Treasure Spirits (Avalonia, 2009)

### David Rankine, with Paul Harry Barron
The Book of Gold (17th century Psalm Magic), (Avalonia, 2010)

### David Rankine, with Stephen Skinner
A Collection of Magical Secrets (Avalonia, 2009)
The Veritable Key of Solomon (Golden Hoard Press, 2008)
The Goetia of Dr Rudd (Golden Hoard Press, 2007)
The Keys to the Gateway of Magic (Golden Hoard Press, 2005)

For more information on these and other titles see:
**www.avaloniabooks.co.uk**

# THE COSMIC SHEKINAH

A historical study of the Goddess of the
Old Testament and Kabbalah

## Sorita d'Este & David Rankine

Published by Avalonia
www.avaloniabooks.co.uk

Published by Avalonia

BM Avalonia, London, WC1N 3XX, England, UK

www.avaloniabooks.co.uk

The Cosmic Shekinah
© Sorita and David Rankine, 2010
All rights reserved.

First Published by Avalonia 2011
ISBN 978-1-905297-51-1

Typeset and design by Satori
Cover Art "White Dove" © iStockPhoto

British Library Cataloguing in Publication Data. A catalogue record for
this book is available from the British Library.

# Acknowledgements

We would like to thank the following people for their assistance with this book:

Jerome Rothenberg for his kind permission to reproduce his translation of Isaac Luria's *Hymn to Shekinah for the Feast of the Sabbath*, first published in *The Secret Garden*, edited by David Meltzer, 1976.

Jerry Buterbaugh and Jon Buckley for sharing insights and information on the Manichean texts; Jonathan Carfax for sharing his resources on the Shekinah; Dr Nina Lazarus for sharing her historical research on Lilith; John Canard for sharing his views on the sacred World Tree;

Miguel Connor, Geoffrey Dennis, William G. Dever, Erik Hornung, Daniel Matt and Peter Schäfer for their excellent and very useful research and writings.

Also: Eva Archer, Paul Harry Barron, Emily Carding, Michael Ellis, Elysia Gallo, Darcy Kuntz, Joseph C. Lisiewski, Stephen Skinner, Mark Townsend and Peter Tunder for their support, encouragement and enthusiasm for our work.

The students of our Qabalah Groups (Abergavenny & London), as well as the fraternity of the O.I.F. for their pertinent questions and perpetual thirst for knowledge which has encouraged us deeper into the mysteries over the years.

*To Geraldine Beskin*
*Fount of Esoteric Wisdom*

# CONTENTS

*"And the Holy Spirit rested upon him, teaching that the Shekinah only rests upon one who is joyful of heart."*

Yalkut on Jonah 1.1

# Naming Wisdom

*"I learnt it all, hidden or manifest,*
*for I was taught by Wisdom,*
*by her whose skill made all things."*
~ *Wisdom of Solomon, C1st BCE, trans. Schäfer.*

The Shekinah is the primordial light of creation, the heavenly glory of divine wisdom and the inspiration for prophecy. She is also the world soul, manifest through the divine sparks of her light which comprise human souls and thus unites us all. With roots in the wisdom goddesses of the ancient world, the Shekinah is the manifestation of feminine divinity from the unnamed Wisdom Goddess of the *Old Testament* found in the Jewish mystical systems known as the Kabbalah and Merkavah mysticism.

The name Shekinah first appeared in material found in the *Onkelos Targum*, which dates from the first-second century CE. This text, by an unknown author, was misnamed during the medieval period after Onkelos the Proselyte (35-110 CE), who translated the Bible into Aramaic. In the *Onkelos Targum* the term Shekinah is used to illustrate a divine presence which is separate from Yahweh, as in the paraphrase of *Exodus 25:8*;

> "And they shall make before me a sanctuary and I shall cause my Shekinah to dwell among them."

9

The first glimpse of the power or function of the Shekinah is seen in the meaning of her name, which is derived from the Hebrew root *Shakhan* meaning *'to dwell'*. This meaning hints at her tangible presence as a visible manifestation of the light of wisdom in the books of the *Old Testament*, as the burning bush seen by Moses, in the Ark of the Covenant and in the Temple of Solomon. Her name was also Aramaized to Shekinta in some texts like the Targums, which are Aramaic translations of the Bible that often included commentaries.

The Shekinah is first hinted at as the unnamed Wisdom Goddess of the books of the *Old Testament*, as well as being named in apocryphal and pseudoepigraphical books from the latter part of this period, spanning a thousand years from the seventh or sixth century BCE through to the third or fourth century CE. Whilst it has been suggested that the Shekinah was simply a hypostasis of God's glory, personifying his qualities, the traces found in these ancient writings make it clear that she was much more than this.

By exploring the myths and deities of the ancient Middle East, it becomes clear that the origins of the Shekinah may be found in several earlier goddesses associated with wisdom in civilizations such as those of Sumer, Egypt and Canaan. From the rich cultural cross-fertilization between these civilizations sprang the Shekinah.

The most prominent and wide-ranging descriptions of the Shekinah, her influence and roles may be found in the teachings of the Kabbalah, and Merkavah (*'Chariot'*) mysticism. Merkavah mysticism is a Jewish system of practices which formed the basis of the Kabbalah, and whose origins may be traced back to around the second century BCE. Merkavah mysticism encouraged the practitioner (called a Merkavah rider) to use amulets, prayers and repetitious chanting of divine names to enable their soul to ascend through the seven palaces or heavens to the presence of God, as described in the Biblical *Book of Ezekiel*.

The main Merkavah texts, called Hekhalot (*'heavenly palace/hall'*) texts were largely written in the period from the third-ninth century CE, and provide many of the richest and most useful descriptions of the Shekinah. These texts include *Book of 3 Enoch* or *Sepher Hekhalot* (C2nd-C6th CE), *Hekhalot Rabbati* (C3rd-C7th CE), *Maaseh Merkavah* (C3rd-C9th CE), *Re'uyot Yehezkiel* (C4th CE) and *Shiur Qoma* (C7th-C12th CE)

Prior to the medieval period the earthly Shekinah was viewed more as the perfection man had lost and strived to regain. She was seen both as the glory of God shining in heaven, and on earth shining forth from the Ark of the Covenant, and as a symbol of the lost Garden of Eden. This is why the pseudoepigraphical *Book of 3 Enoch*, a major early source of Shekinah material (containing sections dating from the second to the sixth century CE) describes the first families of man as dwelling at the gate of Eden to behold the brightness of the Shekinah.[1]

Subtleties of phraseology, often lost in translation, have sometimes hidden the presence of the Shekinah. This has resulted in numerous replacements of the occurrence of the divine feminine, such as the name of the goddess Asherah, the Canaanite predecessor of the Wisdom Goddess (and hence the Shekinah), who is found forty times in the *Old Testament*, her name being translated as *'grove'*, and likewise Shekinah being translated in the *New Testament* as *'tabernacle'*:

> *"And I saw the holy city, the New Jerusalem, coming down out of heaven from God, prepared as a bride adorned for her husband. And I heard a loud voice from the throne saying, 'See, the Shekinah of God is among mortals. He will dwell with them."*[2]

---

1 3 Enoch 5:3, C2nd-C6th CE.
2 Revelations 21:2-3, C1st CE.

At times Israel too was described in the *Old Testament* as the bride of Yahweh, resulting in passages with multiple meanings depending on which interpretation the reader decided on. These writings demonstrate the shift away from the Canaanite goddess Asherah as the consort of Yahweh, emphasised by the strictures against her in books such as *1 Kings*, *2 Kings* and *Deuteronomy*. This process took centuries, as may be seen by such textual references and in archaeological evidence, which we will explore in the chapter *From Canaan*.

Following the ongoing removal of the worship of Asherah from the Hebrew tribes, we see the unnamed Wisdom Goddess effectively replacing Asherah as the divine bride. This is made clear in the third century BCE writings of *Proverbs* and contemporary Jewish wisdom literature, which is several centuries later than the biblical books containing Asherah references which date more to the period of seventh-sixth century BCE.

The Wisdom Goddess (and later the Shekinah) may initially seem a more discrete partner for Yahweh, emphasising wisdom rather than such challenging powers as fertility and sexuality, which were associated with Asherah. However this did not entirely succeed, as can be seen by the erotic nature of the Biblical *Song of Solomon*, which has some very explicit symbolism woven into its beautiful verses, and also by the sexual symbolism later associated with the Shekinah in the Kabbalah.

The transition from unnamed Wisdom Goddess to named divine feminine wisdom as the Shekinah occurred around first-second century CE, contemporary with the *Gospels*, the earliest Merkavah texts (such as the *Revelation of Moses*), the first Kabbalistic text (*Sepher Yetzirah*) and the proliferation of Gnostic texts. From the moment when the Shekinah is named as the divine feminine wisdom, her influence may be seen again and again in subsequent centuries, expressed through such phenomenon as the Holy Spirit and the power of prophecy, and found in religious, magical and poetic writings.

Prior to the Wisdom Goddess and Asherah, we will also explore the significance of wisdom goddesses in earlier civilizations such as those of Sumer, ancient Egypt and Canaan, and demonstrate the significant influence and cultural cross-fertilisation that occurred through their contact with the Semitic tribes. In so doing we illustrate the enduring presence of the divine feminine wisdom in human cultures spanning thousands of years, which endures today in the Shekinah.

# Timeline of Texts

References in brackets indicate that the goddess is implied by title or description if not specifically named.

| Time | Work | Goddess Reference |
|---|---|---|
| C30th-C20th BCE | Inanna and the God of Wisdom | Inanna |
| C30th-C20th BCE | The Huluppu Tree | Inanna, Lilith |
| C24th BCE | Hymn to Inanna – Enheduanna | Inanna |
| C21st-C20th BCE | The Epic of Gilgamesh | Inanna, Siduri |
| C14th-C13th BCE | Canaanite/Ugaritic Myths including A Hymn to Anat, The RPUM Texts, The Plea for a House for Baal, An Incantation for the Exorcism of a Possessed Adolescent | Asherah, Anat |
| C11th-C8th BCE | The Writings of Sakkunyaton (lost) | Astarte, Aphrodite |
| C10th-C8th BCE | Book of Genesis | Eve |
| C10th-C8th BCE | Book of Exodus | Asherah, (Shekinah) |
| C10th-C8th BCE | Book of Samuel | - |
| C10th-C2nd BCE | Book of Psalms | (Shekinah) |
| C8th BCE | Theogony – Hesiod | Hekate, Metis, Athena |
| C8th BCE | Book of Judges | Anat, Asherah, Astarte, Deborah |
| C8th-C7th BCE | Book of Micah | Asherah |
| C8th-C5th BCE | Book of Numbers | - |
| C7th BCE | Book of Jeremiah | Asherah, Inanna |
| C7th BCE | Book of 1 Kings | Asherah |
| C7th BCE | Book of 2 Kings | Asherah |

14

| | | |
|---|---|---|
| C7th-C6th BCE | Book of Deuteronomy | Asherah |
| C7th-C6th BCE | Book of Isaiah | Asherah, Lilith |
| C7th-C6th BCE | Book of Joshua | Anat |
| C6th BCE | Book of Ezekiel | (Asherah) |
| C6th BCE | Book of Lamentations | - |
| C6th BCE | Book of Zechariah | (Shekinah) |
| C5th BCE | Tetrasomia (Doctrine of Four Elements) – Empedocles | Aphrodite |
| C4th BCE | Phaedo – Plato | (Earth) |
| C4th BCE | Timaeus – Plato | (Earth) |
| C4th – C2nd BCE | Book of Ecclesiastes | (Shekinah) |
| C3rd BCE | Book of Job | (Shekinah) |
| C3rd BCE | Book of Proverbs | (Shekinah) |
| C3rd BCE | Book of 2 Chronicles | Asherah |
| C3rd - C2nd BCE | Song of Solomon | (Shekinah) |
| C2nd BCE | Book of Baruch | Edem |
| C2nd BCE | Jesus Sirach – Ben Sira | Wisdom Goddess |
| C2nd BCE – C5th CE | Greek Magical Papyri | Hekate, (Barbelo) |
| C1st BCE | Wisdom of Solomon | Wisdom Goddess |
| C1st CE | Haggigah | (Shekinah) |
| C1st CE | De Cherubim - Philo of Alexandria | Wisdom Goddess |
| C1st CE | Book of Revelation | (Shekinah) |
| C1st CE | Book of 2 Corinthians | - |
| C1st-C2nd CE | The Gospels of Matthew, Mark, Luke & John | (Shekinah) |
| C1st-C2nd CE | The Book of 1 Peter | - |
| C1st-C2nd CE | Onkelos Targum | Shekinah |
| C1st-C3rd CE | Gedulath Mosheh (The Revelation of Moses) | Shekinah |
| C2nd CE | De Dea Syria (Of The Syrian Goddess) – Lucian of Samosata | Astarte, Ashtoreth, Ishtar |
| C2nd CE | Sepher Yetzirah (The Book of Formation) | (Shekinah) |
| C2nd CE- | Testament of Solomon | Obizuth (/Lilith) |

| | | |
|---|---|---|
| C2nd CE | Sanhedrin | Shekinah |
| C2nd CE | Acts of Thomas | Sophia (Shekinah) |
| C2nd CE | Apocryphon of John | Sophia & Barbelo |
| C2nd CE | The Book of James (Protevangelium) | Mary |
| C2nd CE | The Odes of Solomon | Wisdom Goddess |
| C2nd CE | Chaldean Oracles of Zoroaster | Hekate, Physis |
| C2nd CE | Against Heresies - Iraneus | Sophia, Ennoia |
| C2nd CE | Refutation of All Heresies – Hippolytus | Paraclete (Holy Spirit) |
| C2nd CE | Metamorphoses (Golden Ass) – Apuleius | Isis |
| C2nd-C6th CE | Book of 3 Enoch, also called Sepher Hekhalot (Book of the Palaces) | Shekinah |
| C3rd CE | Mishnah (Instruction) | Shekinah |
| C3rd CE | Symposia – Methodius of Lucian Olympus | (Heaven) |
| C3rd CE | On Abstinence – Porphyry | Hekate |
| C3rd CE | Pistis Sophia | Sophia, Mary |
| C3rd-C4th CE | The Thunder, Perfect Mind | Sophia |
| C3rd-C7th CE | Hekhalot Rabbati (The Greater Palaces) | Shekinah |
| C3rd-C9th CE | Maaseh Merkavah (The Work of the Chariot) | Shekinah |
| C4th CE | Re'uyot Yehezkiel (Visions of Ezekiel) | Shekinah |
| C4th CE | The Apocalypse of Adam | Sophia, Eve |
| C4th CE | The Apocalypse of Zostrianos | Barbelo |
| C4th CE | The First Apocalypse of James | Sophia |
| C4th CE | The Hypostasis of the Archons | Sophia |
| C4th CE | Melchizidek | Barbelo |
| C4th CE | On the Origin of the World | Sophia, Eve |
| C4th CE | The Second Treatise of the Great Seth | Sophia |
| C4th CE | The Sophia of Jesus Christ | Sophia, Eve |
| C4th CE | Trimorphic Protennoia | Barbelo |
| C4th CE | Hymns – St Ephrem | Shekinah |
| C4th-C5th CE | Homilies & Recognitions – Pseudo-Clement | Luna/Helen (as Wisdom) |
| C5th CE | Homiliae Diversae (Diverse sermons) – Cyril of Alexandria | Mary |

| | | |
|---|---|---|
| C5th-C6th CE | Pesikta de Rav-Kahana (The verses of Rabbi Kahana) | Shekinah |
| C6th CE | Pseudo-Melito | Mary (as Shekinah) |
| C6th CE | Akathist Hymn to the Theotokos | Mary (as Shekinah) |
| C7th CE | The Qur'an | Sakina |
| C7th-C12th CE | Shiur Qoma (Measure of the Height) | Shekinah |
| C8th-C10th CE | Turfan Fragments | Sophia |
| C8th-C10th CE | Alphabet of Ben Sirra | Lilith |
| C10th CE | Sepher 'Emunoth we-De'oth (The Book of Beliefs and Opinions) – Saadia Gaon | Shekinah |
| C11th CE | The Thirty-Two Paths of Wisdom | (Shekinah) |
| C12th CE | Kuzari – Judah Halevi | Shekinah |
| C12th CE | Bahir | Shekinah |
| C12th CE | Commentary on Sepher Yetzirah – Judah ben Barzillai | Shekinah |
| C12th CE | Sepher Ha-Ma'or ha-Gadol (The Book of the Great Luminary) - Zerachiah ha-Levi of Gerona | Shekinah |
| C12th CE | Moreh Nevuchim (Guide for the Perplexed) – Moses Maimonides | Shekinah |
| C12th CE | Yesodey HaTorah (Mishnah of the Torah) | Tree of Life |
| C12th CE | Symphonia & other writings – Hildegard von Bingen | Mary (as Shekinah), Holy Spirit (as Sophia /Shekinah) |
| C13th CE | Zohar | Shekinah, Lilith |
| C13th CE | Hokmath ha-Egoz (The Wisdom of the Nut) - Eleazer of Worms | Shekinah |
| C13th CE | Sepher ha-Hokhmah (The Book of Wisdom) – Eleazer of Worms | Shekinah |
| C13th CE | Treatise on the Left Emanation – Rabbi Isaac | Lilith |
| C13th CE | The Book of the Bee – Solomon of Akhlat | (Shekinah) |

| | | |
|---|---|---|
| C13th CE | Sepher Chaije Olam Ha-ba (The Book of the Life of the World to Come) – Abraham Abulafia | Shekinah |
| C13th CE | Get Ha-Shemot (Divorce of the Names) – Abraham Abulafia | (Shekinah) |
| C13th CE | Or HaShekhal (Light of the Intellect) – Abraham Abulafia | (Shekinah) |
| C13th CE | Sepher Ha-Ot (Book of the Sign) – Abraham Abulafia | Shekinah |
| C13th CE | Shaar HaKavanah (The Gate of Kavanah) – Azriel of Gerona | (Shekinah) |
| C13th CE | Sepher Mar'ot Hazove'ot (Book of Mirrors) - David ben Judah Hehasid | Shekinah |
| C13th CE | Sepher Raziel (Book of Raziel) | Shekinah |
| C13th CE | Heptameron (Seven Days) – Peter de Abano | Paraclete |
| C14th CE | Sepher Shekel haKodesh (The Book of the Holy Coin) – Moses de Leon | Shekinah |
| C14th CE | Tur (Row) – Jacob Ben Asher | Tree of Life |
| C15th CE | Homilies – Ephraim Ben Gershon | Shekinah |
| C16th CE | Hymn to the Shekinah – Isaac Luria | Shekinah |
| C16th CE | Shaarei Kedusha (Gates of Holiness) – Chaim Vital | Shekinah |
| C16th CE | The Second Call – John Dee & Edward Kelley | (Shekinah) |
| C17th CE | Or ha-Hayyim – Azulai | Shekinah |
| C17th CE | The Chemical Wedding of Christian Rosenkreutz | (Shekinah) |
| C17th CE | Goetia | Paraclete |
| C17th CE | Shecinah: or a Demonstration of the Divine Presence in the Places of Religious Worship – John Stillingfleet | Shekinah |
| C17th CE | The Moral Schechinah: or a Discourse on God's Glory – George Hickes | Shekinah |
| C17th CE | Christian Life – J Scott | Shekinah |
| C18th CE | Mesillat Yesharim – Moses Luzatto | Shekinah |

| | | |
|---|---|---|
| C18th CE | Hymn on the Titles of Christ – Wesley | Shekinah as Jesus |
| C19th CE | The Revelation of the Shechinah – Frederick Holland | Shekinah |
| C19th CE | Chtenia – Vladimir Solov'ev | Shekinah, Sophia |

## Note:

All quotes from the Torah are taken from *The Living Torah*, translated by Aryeh Kaplan. All quotes from the remainder of the *Old Testament*, and any from the *New Testament*, are taken from the *New Revised Standard Version of the Bible*.

The abbreviation KAI refers to the book *Kanaanäische und Aramäische Inscriften*, which lists and describes numerous inscriptions from the ancient Middle East.

In this work we distinguish between the Jewish system of Kabbalah and its derivatives by spelling. When the spelling of Qabalah is used, it refers to the modern (non-Jewish) magical system derived from the Kabbalah, and the spelling of Cabalah refers to the specifically Christian derivative of the Kabbalah.

The spellings of Qabalistic terms such as Sephiroth and their names are given in the Anglicized forms of their transliterations throughout rather than the Jewish.

# Part 1

# The Shekinah Unveiled

# Manifestations

> *"Anyone who recites this prayer with all his strength can behold the radiance of the Shekinah and he is the beloved of the Shekinah."*
> ~ *Synopse 591, Hekhalot Rabbati, C3rd-C7th CE*

## She is the Serpent ...

The relationship between the Shekinah and the serpent is significant, particularly in light of the ambivalent nature of the symbolism associated with serpents in different cultures. Considering other wisdom goddesses, the serpent motif recurs with a number of them. For instance the Canaanite wisdom and mother goddess Asherah was known as the lady of the serpent (*dāt baṭni*). The serpent motif is of course a common one in many cultures, and it is the serpent that tempts Eve to gain wisdom in the *Book of Genesis*, a course of action sometimes equated with initiation into wisdom.

Images of the Egyptian goddess Qudshu, who was associated with Asherah, frequently show her holding serpents. There are sixteen or so Egyptian plaques from the New Kingdom (sixteenth-eleventh century BCE) showing

Qudshu (also called Qadesh)[3] standing on a lion, holding lotuses in her right hand and a serpent in her left hand.

Furthermore, it is interesting to note that the Greek goddess Hekate (who has parallels to the Shekinah as world soul, source of souls and many other motifs) also had snake symbolism associated with her on numerous occasions, including in the *Greek Magical Papyri* (C2nd BCE-C5th CE) and as the wisdom goddess of the *Chaldean Oracles* (C2nd CE).[4]

The Gnostic goddess Edem, a form of Sophia and hence also associated with wisdom, bears what is probably the strongest serpentine imagery. She is depicted as being half human and half serpent; and as we will show, this is undoubtedly derived from earlier sources such as the Greek mythical Echidna or the Egyptian goddess Isis-Hermouthis. In the creation myth as told in the second century BCE *Book of Baruch*, the third of the twelve angels created by Edem was Naas ('snake'), who equates to the serpent of wisdom on the Tree in the garden of Eden, again emphasising her very strong relationship with serpents.

# She is the Dove ...

The dove is one of the most enduring symbols of the Shekinah. Traditionally the dove is associated with goddesses of love in the ancient world, including the Phoenician goddess Astarte and the Canaanite goddess Asherah, both of whom are wisdom goddesses and both of whom are historically and symbolically linked with the Shekinah. The relationship between the Wisdom Goddess and the dove is found repeatedly in the beautiful *Song of Solomon*, most poignantly in the Kabbalistically rich symbolism of verse 5:2:

---

3 The Religions of Israel, Zevit, 2003:323.
4 See Hekate Liminal Rites, d'Este & Rankine, 2009:141-2.

*"I slept, but my heart was awake.*
*Listen! my beloved is knocking.*
*'Open to me, my sister, my love,*
*my dove, my perfect one;*
*for my head is wet with dew,*
*my locks with the drops of the night.'"*

According to the book of *Genesis*, dew is the water of the heavens, the living water which was divided from earthly water when creation occurred. The reference to dew can, from a Kabbalistic perspective, be interpreted as Kether, the highest Sephira, which echoes the reference to the Shekinah and the Supernal Triad of the Sephiroth of Kether, Chokmah and Binah found in *Proverbs 3:19-20*:

*"The Lord by wisdom [the Sephira of Chokmah as the Shekinah] founded the earth; by understanding [the Sephira of Binah as the Shekinah] he established the heavens; by his knowledge [the false Sephira of Daath as the gateway] the deeps broke open, and the clouds drop down the dew."*[5]

There are additional references in the *Song of Solomon* which further emphasises the dove as being symbolic of the Wisdom Goddess. These examples further accentuate both her beauty and her voice:

*"Behold, thou art fair, my love; behold, thou art fair; thou hast doves' eyes."*[6]

*"O my dove, that art in the clefts of the rock, in the secret places of the stairs, let me see thy countenance, let me hear thy voice; for sweet is thy voice, and thy countenance is comely."*[7]

---

5 Proverbs 3:19-20, C3rd BCE.
6 Song of Solomon 1:15, C3rd-C2nd BCE.
7 Song of Solomon 2:14, C3rd-C2nd BCE.

> *"Behold, thou art fair, my love; behold, thou art fair; thou hast doves' eyes within thy locks:"*[8]

> *"My dove, my undefiled is but one; she is the only one of her mother"*[9]

The Holy Spirit is also likened to a dove, as seen in the Gospels when she descends on Jesus at his baptism in the river Jordan by John the Baptist (*Matthew 3:16, Mark 1:10, Luke 3:22, John 1:32*). Additionally, this theme is found in Gnostic texts, such as *Pistis Sophia*, in comments where Sophia is equated to the Holy Spirit, such as *"my father sent me the holy spirit in the type of a dove"*.[10]

Furthermore, the dove is also frequently associated with feminine wisdom in the form of Sophia in other Gnostic texts. In the following example from the *Odes of Solomon*, Sophia comes to Jesus in the form of a dove singing over him:

> *"The dove fluttered over the head of our Lord Messiah, because He was her head. And she sang over Him, and her voice was heard."*[11]

Turning to the Gnostic text *The Acts of Thomas,* we find numerous symbols attributed to Sophia, including many symbols commonly associated with the Shekinah, such as light, fragrance and the dove:

> *"Come, she that manifesteth the hidden things and maketh the unspeakable things plain, the holy dove."*[12]

---

8 Song of Solomon 4:1, C3rd-C2nd BCE.
9 Song of Solomon 6:9, C3rd-C2nd BCE.
10 Pistis Sophia, 373, C3rd CE.
11 Odes of Solomon, 24, C2nd CE, trans. J.H. Charlesworth.
12 The Acts of Thomas, 50, C2nd CE, trans. M.R. Charles

The Virgin Mary as a key figure of feminine wisdom, who may have been influenced by the Shekinah, is also symbolised by the dove. This is demonstrated in the *Book of James*, where the Virgin Mary is likened to a dove. In this context it suggests her inherent perfection as the future mother of Jesus:

> *"And Mary was in the temple of the Lord as a dove that is nurtured: and she received food from the hand of an angel."*[13]

The Holy Spirit/Shekinah as a dove may also be seen as a motif in alchemy in the Middle Ages and the Renaissance. The second image in the famous alchemical series in *Rosarium Philosophorum* from 1550 CE shows how her influence permeated the esoteric disciplines.[14] Between the two crowned figures, of a king standing on the sun and the queen standing on the moon, we see a dove beneath a six-rayed star holding a rose (another wisdom emblem) in its beak which is touching the king's sleeve. Significantly, this sequence is one which revolves around the theme of the alchemical process of unification, recalling the aim of unification of the Heavenly and Earthly Shekinah.

# She is the Burning Bush ...

A story of the first century religious teacher Rabbi Gamaliel records that when he was asked why God revealed himself in a burning bush to Moses, he replied *"To teach you there is no place on earth not occupied by the Shekinah, that is, there is no place on earth where the Shekinah cannot reveal itself."*[15]

---

13 The Book of James, 8.1, C2nd CE, trans. M.R. James.
14 De Alchimia opuscula complura veterum philosophorum, Frankfurt, 1550 CE.
15 Pesikta de Rav-Kahana 2b (Verse of Rav Kahana), C5th-C6th CE.

The idea that it was the Shekinah who spoke to Moses from the burning bush is a common one in old Kabbalistic texts. As the Shekinah was equated to both of the prophetic mediums of the Ruach HaQadosh (*'spirit of holiness'*) and the Bath Kol (*'daughter of the voice'*), it is easy to see why the burning bush should be considered as one of her manifestations. The burning fires of the bush also hints at the divine fires associated with the Shekinah in many of the descriptions of her.

The encounters between Moses and the divine glory are one of the key introductions to the Shekinah in the *Old Testament*. Thus when *"God's glory rested on Mount Sinai"*,[16] the word for glory is *Kavod*, which is commonly equated to and replaced by Shekinah in commentaries on the *Old Testament*, and the word for *'rested'* is *shakan*, the root of Shekinah.

The burning bush is an example of an occurrence described in some texts as *Gilluy Shekinah*, which is a divine manifestation by a wondrous act which overawes the recipient with the glory of its presence. Gilluy Shekinah is thus a manifestation of the Greater Shekinah.

# She is the Tree of Life

The whole Tree of Life was often described as being a symbol of the Shekinah in medieval Kabbalistic writings. From the common symbolism of the Asherah pole seen in the ancient Canaanite and Hebrew world, in such declarations as, *"they set up for themselves pillars and sacred poles [Asherim] on every high hill and under every green tree; there they made offerings on all the high places"*[17] it is clear that the carved figure of a symbolic Tree of Life and then subsequently the glyph of the Qabalistic Tree of

---

16 Exodus 24:16, C10th-C8th BCE.
17 2 Kings 17:10-11, C7th BCE.

Life have always been associated with the goddess of wisdom.

Indeed the Tree of Life, or World Tree, is a common motif, found in numerous cultures such as ancient Egypt, Sumer and Canaan, as well as the biblical Tree of Life found in *Genesis* and *Proverbs*. From these origins may stem the cosmological tree of life of the Qabalah, which has been equated to the Shekinah both in part and as a whole.

The goddess Asherah was particularly associated with the palm tree, as seen by archaeological references throughout the Middle East. It is interesting that the palm tree should then come to have such a significant symbolic presence in the ceremonies of both Judaism and Christianity, though of course as a self-sustaining tree in a harsh environment it was an essential aid to survival.

The etrog or yellow citron tree (*citrus medica*), as a symbolic representation of the Shekinah is described in a parable in the Kabbalistic text of the *Bahir* (172), where the king planted nine male palms, and then a female etrog to ensure their survival (representing Malkuth as the tenth and purely feminine Sephira, the Earthly Shekinah).

Titles for the Virgin Mary which may have drawn from these associations with Asherah include some of those found in the sixth century *Akathist Hymn to the Theotokos* such as the *'well-shaded Tree'* and *'tree of delectable Fruit'* mentioned in the Russian and Greek Orthodox Churches.

# She is invoked with incense smoke...

The burning of incense was practiced throughout the ancient world as part of the worship of the gods. However there is a dichotomy in the *Old Testament*, with both recipes for incense and injunctions not to burn incense being given. What is meant is that incense should not be burned to other gods apart from Yahweh, and that it should not be burned in high places because of its association to the goddess Asherah. Hence the critical reference in the *Book of 1 Kings* that *"Solomon loved the Lord (Yahweh), walking in the statutes of his father David; only, he sacrificed and offered incense at the high places."*[18]

The burning of incense was a widespread and regular part of Asherah worship, and we can speculate that the four horns of the altar/incense burner could represent the four directions, or four phases of the moon, or other quaternary symbolism. The four horned incense burners are described in the Bible, with a flat square top with the horns on each corner, and can be dated back to at least the tenth century BCE, such as those found at Megiddo (i.e. to the pre-monotheistic period). We know from archaeological evidence that such burners were sometimes used exclusively for incense, e.g. a burner found at Lachish (in the kingdom of Judah) had the word for frankincense (*lbnt*) inscribed on it in Aramaic.

Indeed fourteen references are made in the *Old Testament* to horned altars which are used for sacrificing animals on, as well as burning incense on.[19] The burning of incense was also associated with the burnt offerings made to Yahweh, and significantly was believed to help draw the presence of the Shekinah:

> *"Because the act of sacrifice is meant for its own sake and is extremely useful, since it brings the Shekinah to dwell among those who know how to attract the supreme power through the pleasant odour, and they know what is to come."*[20]

---

18 1 Kings 3:3, C7th BCE.

19 Exodus 29:12,37:25; Leviticus 4:7, 4:18, 8:15, 9:9, 16:18; 1 Kings 1:50, 2:28; Psalms 118:27; Jeremiah 17:1; Ezekiel 43:15, 43:20; Amos 3:14.

20 Sepher Ha-Ma'or ha-Gadol, Zerachiah ha-Levi of Girona (1125-1186), 167b, C12th CE.

Reference to the attractive power of sacrifice is also found in the fourteenth century text *Or Adonai*, in which it is acknowledged that:

> "*Through the sacrifices, those bringing the offerings will attain the emanation, the abundance, and a perceptible and imperceptible conjunction with the light of the Shekinah, to the point where they will sometimes feel the fire's descent from Heaven.*"[21]

The Gnostics too were aware of the attraction of the divine wisdom through fragrance, implied in connection with Sophia in the *Wedding Hymn* in the *Acts of Thomas*, which proclaims:

> "*Her bridal chamber is full of light, breathing a scent of balsam and every spice, giving off a sweet fragrance of myrrh and silphium, and of all kinds of sweet-smelling flowers*"[22]

It is not just through the use of incense that the link between the divine and fragrance is made. In the writings of the early Christian mystics the connection between perfume and heavenly paradise as a beautiful garden (i.e. Eden, the manifest Earthly Shekinah) was often emphasised. For example, in the third century CE Saint Methodius recorded in his heavenly vision that:

> "*The ever-blossoming meadows, too, were dotted with all kinds of sweet-scented flowers, and from them there was wafted a gentle breeze laden with perfume.*"[23]

Kabbalists believed that celebrating the Sabbath brought the parts of the soul together, and that fragrances

---

21 Or Adonai, Hasdai Crescas (1340-1410), printed 1555.
22 The Wedding Hymn, Acts of Thomas, 12-13, C2nd CE.
23 Symposia, Methodius, C3rd CE.

sustained them when they were again separated during the rest of the week, as seen by references in the *Zohar*, such as the tale of Rabbi Yose, Rabbi Abba and the rose. This doctrine of the disjunction of the parts of the soul formed the basis for one of the key philosophies of the Kabbalah, i.e. uniting the different parts of the soul to achieve greater wisdom and spiritual awareness.

# She is the Precious Jewel ...

The *Bahir* contains a number of parables which liken the Shekinah to precious jewels and stones. Thus she is the *'beautiful pearl'* owned by the king (God) which he embraces and kisses when he is happy and loves. It is interesting to note that he places the pearl on his head, as this is the position of the crown, symbolic of kingship.

> *"A king had a beautiful pearl, and it was the treasure of his kingdom. When he is happy, he embraces it, kisses it, places it on his head, and loves it."* [24]

Malkuth (and hence the Shekinah) is known as a precious stone due to the fact that it receives and reflects the emanations of all the other Sephiroth on the Tree of Life. The Shekinah is also referred to in the fourth vision of Zechariah as the *"stone with seven eyes (or facets)"*,[25] referring to the seven lower Sephiroth on the Tree of Life, the seven classical planets and the seven days of creation.

---

24 Bahir, 72 C12th CE.
25 Zechariah 3:9, C6th BCE.

# She is the Lily ...

One of the best known verses in the *Song of Solomon* starts with *"I am a rose of Sharon, a lily of the valleys. As a lily among brambles, so is my love among maidens"*[26] illustrating both the beautiful prose of the *Song of Solomon* and the association of the Wisdom Goddess with lilies. There are six other references in the *Song of Solomon* to lilies, amongst which we find the line *"My beloved is mine and I am his; he pastures his flock among the lilies."*[27] In this instance, the lily is then also equated with Yahweh, suggesting a degree of exchange of symbolism between the divine bride and groom, thus, *"His lips are lilies, distilling liquid myrrh."*[28]

Another interesting reference hinting at the Shekinah is found in the opening lines of *Psalm 80*, which specifically mentions lilies:

> *"To the leader: on Lilies, a Covenant. Of Asaph. A Psalm.*
> *Give ear, O Shepherd of Israel, you who lead Joseph like a flock! ... You who are enthroned upon the cherubim, shine forth"*[29]

The Shekinah is the one who is enthroned upon the Cherubim, who shines forth. Moreover the Pillars in the Temple of Solomon which correspond to the Black and White Pillars on the Tree of Life were described as having lilies crowning the capitals on them,[30] emphasising the divine wisdom of the Shekinah (as Binah and Chokmah, the Sephiroth at the top of those two pillars on the Tree of Life).

---

26 Song of Solomon 2:1-2, C3rd-C2nd BCE.
27 Song of Solomon 2:16, C3rd-C2nd BCE.
28 Song of Solomon 5:13, C3rd-C2nd BCE.
29 Psalm 80:1-2, C10th-C2nd BCE.
30 1 Kings 7:19-22, C7th BCE.

Medieval Church figures such as Hildegard von Bingen would also use lily symbolism in association with the Virgin Mary when portraying her as the redemptrix, and emphasising her divinity (and hence her implied connection to the Holy Spirit or Shekinah). By doing so, the Virgin Mary's function became conflated with that of the Shekinah, and she was given a pre-creation role as *"the shining white lily on which God gazed before all creation."*[31] This position before creation directly equates the Virgin Mary to the Wisdom Goddess from a biblical perspective and the Shekinah from a Kabbalistic perspective.

# She sits on the Throne of Glory

The Throne of Glory is the centre of an epic spiritual quest which forms the basis of a school of Jewish mysticism which influenced the Kabbalah, called Merkavah mysticism. Merkavah (meaning *'chariot'*) mysticism is based on the idea that with sufficient preparation and purification, a Merkavah rider can ascend through the seven palaces (which correspond to the seven classical planets and the lower Sephiroth on the Qabalistic Tree of Life) to enter the presence of God, where he sits on the Throne of Glory. This is derived from the vision described in the first verse of the *Book of Ezekiel*, and a collection of literature known as the *Hekhalot* (*'palace'*) texts, which includes the *Book of 3 Enoch*.

Significantly there is reference to more than one Throne in some of the texts like *3 Enoch*, with one for God and/or one for the Shekinah (as in the fourth century CE Merkavah text *Re'uyot Yehezkiel*). We should also remember that the name of the ancient Egyptian goddess  Isis meant *'throne'*, and her symbol was a throne, so it is possible that her influence as a wisdom goddess was a contributory factor to the development of this path. Some

---

31 Symphonia, Hildegard of Bingen, 1170 CE.

scholars have also suggested the Isian influence, such as MacRae, who commented that he believed the origin of the Jewish concept of wisdom (the Shekinah) can be found in *"the late Jewish tendency toward the hypostatization of divine attributes and the widespread ancient myths of the female deity, especially the Isis myths"*.[32]

The controversial and to some blasphemous text *Shiur Qoma* (Measure of the Height), which gives the dimensions of God's body (and hence describes the indescribable), includes an interesting reference to the Shekinah and the Throne of Glory, saying that:

> *"The angels that are with Metatron come and surround the Throne of Glory, they on one side, Chaioth [the highest angels] on the other, and the Shekinah on the Shekinah of Glory in the middle."*[33]

# She dwelt in the Ark of the Covenant

The Ark of the Covenant is one of the many items, like the High Priest's Breastplate, the menorah, the incense burner, the holy incenses and oils, for which detailed instructions for construction are provided in the *Old Testament*. What is particularly significant about this is that, apart from possibly the High Priest's Breastplate, all of these essential items in the worship of God are also associated with the Shekinah.

The Ark of the Covenant is described in *Exodus 25*. Its most significant feature is the two golden cherubim on top of it. Remembering that the Shekinah was said to reside on a Cherubim at the base of the Tree of Life, the association between the Shekinah and the Ark of the Covenant becomes apparent. The Shekinah is associated with

---

32 The Jewish Background of the Gnostic Sophia Myth, MacRae, 87.
33 Shiur Qoma, 9, C7th-C12th CE.

Cherubim in a number of writings, and the references in Jewish texts to the golden statues of the Cherubs embracing at particular times emphasises the divine nature of the Ark as one of her residences.

By the sixth century CE we find that the title *"Ark made golden by the Spirit"* being applied to the Virgin Mary, demonstrating a syncretisation with the Shekinah. This is an interesting parallel, as Mary is effectively being described as the Ark for the divine presence of Jesus, whereas the Ark of the Covenant houses the divine presence of the Shekinah.

The medieval German Pietist Jews expressed an interesting perception of the view of the relationship between the Ark and the Shekinah, with the twelfth century figure of Hezekiah writing:

> *"That one bows before a Torah scroll not because of any inherent Godliness in the Torah itself, but rather because the Shekinah dwells within the Holy Ark. A mystical tradition embraced and expanded upon by the German Pietists identified the Torah with the Divine glory, the Kavod."[34]*

# She dwelt in the Temple of Solomon

The Temple of Solomon was built as a dwelling place for wisdom, which Yahweh had bestowed on Solomon in abundance. A suggested interpretation of *Psalm 118:22*, *"The stone that the builders rejected has become the chief cornerstone"* is that the previous rejection of the stone was the rejection of the Wisdom Goddess, who Solomon then embraced. Solomon was given wisdom by God, which could be interpreted, as some theologians have, to signify that the

---

34 Peering Through the Lattices, Kanarfogel, 2000:161.

Shekinah was given as bride to Solomon, who built his temple to honour wisdom as the divine feminine bride.

King Solomon reigned from 977-927 BCE, and according to the second century CE *Testament of Solomon* used demons to help build the temple. Whilst this may seem extraordinary or even unbelievable today, we should remember that Solomon was famous throughout the ancient world as a great magician, maybe even the greatest. Christian, Jewish and Islamic stories all tell of his renowned ability to call and bind demons. Historical sources provide us with tales of strange phenomena every time the temple was rebuilt after being destroyed, hinting at its supernatural foundations. St Cyril of Jerusalem recorded details of the final attempt to rebuild the temple in May 363 CE, during which there were numerous inexplicable accidents, mysterious fireballs, and finally a substantial earthquake which caused devastation in the surrounding area but left the temple area untouched.[35]

In more recent centuries the Temple of Solomon became the template for the Temple of the Freemasons. Considering the presence of the Shekinah in Solomon's Temple, this then implies that the influence of the Shekinah pervades Freemasonry, a point made by Mark Stavish in his book *Freemasonry: Rituals, Symbols & History of the Secret Society* (2007). The Wisdom Goddess's symbolism, as exemplified through the mythos, pillars and architecture, can still be found as forming the foundations of modern Freemason temples, illustrating her all-pervading influence.

# She is Eternal Light

The most apparent visible motif of the Shekinah is that of light. The association is seen in numerous descriptions of her radiance, her manifestations (e.g. as the burning bush),

---

35 For more details see The Goetia of Dr Rudd, Skinner & Rankine, 2007:20-23.

and her role as the primordial light of creation in Kabbalistic cosmology.

Light is an obvious symbol for wisdom, representing the illumination that results from the insights and realisations gained from wisdom. The prevalence of light, and accordingly fire as a source of light, in the ancient world, has ensured that it is a common attribution for many significant and powerful deities. An example of this theme of divine light is seen in ancient Greece, where *"brightness was linked with divine epiphanies in the Homeric poems, and often assumed concrete forms, such as the lamp of Athena, to express divine power in human terms".*[36]

Today the symbolism of the light of the Shekinah is seen most clearly in the two candles lit at Jewish Shabbat ceremonies round the world every Friday evening, and the Menorah candlestick with its sevenfold and tenfold symbolisms.

# She is Wisdom, the Saviour

It would perhaps be more appropriate to rephrase this section title to say *'Wisdom Goddess as saviour, with a Creator God husband/father'*. This theme recurs through a number of mythologies, and may indicate patterns of cultural influence or simply represent manifestations of particular universal themes in different civilizations.

However in order of antiquity we see the theme of Creator God with Wisdom Goddess as daughter or bride in a number of cultures, including:

- the Sumerian Enki and Inanna,
- the Egyptian Ra and Isis-Ma'at,
- the Canaanite El and Asherah,

---

36 The Light of the Gods, Parisinou, 2000:162.

- the Hebrew Yahweh and Asherah,
- the Hebrew Yahweh and the Wisdom Goddess,
- the Gnostic God and Sophia,
- the Chaldean Zeus and Hekate,
- the Hebrew Yahweh and Shekinah.

In each instance there is a clear salvation theme associated with the feminine divine, thus Inanna presents the *me* (powers) to her people in Uruk; Isis-Ma'at represents truth, justice and natural balance and is frequently described as a saviour figure; Asherah is the Mother of the Gods and dispenser of wisdom; the Wisdom Goddess is co-creatrix with Yahweh and bestower of wisdom; Hekate is the cosmic world soul and speaker of truth who is known as Soteira (saviour); Sophia is the creatrix of the world and bringer of wisdom; and the Shekinah is the world soul and source of primordial light and divine wisdom. All of these goddesses, with their possible links to the Shekinah or similarities in motifs and symbols will be discussed in the following chapters.

# Behind the Veils

*"Her ways are ways of pleasantness,*
*and all her paths are peace.*
*She is a tree of life to those who lay hold of her;*
*those who hold her fast are called happy."*
~ *Proverbs 3:17-18, C3rd BCE*

Through considering the religions which influenced and were influenced by the development of Judaism and the Kabbalah we find not only the origins of the Shekinah, but also her subsequent manifestations. Millennia before the rise of the Shekinah, we see the earliest association between wisdom and feminine divinity in the form of Inanna, the Sumerian goddess of love and war. In the myths of Sumer, southern Mesopotamia, amongst the world's first civilizations, it is Inanna who was said to have given civilization to mankind.

The Sumerian civilization was subsequently replaced by the Akkadians, Babylonians and Assyrians through conquest and cultural assimilation. A result of this process was the renaming of deities as cosmologies were syncretised and transformed through religious cross-fertilisation. The first dynasties of Ancient Egypt were contemporary with the civilization of Sumer. While Sumer underwent transformations through conquest and decline, the Egyptians continued to develop many of the inventions of the Sumerians, such as agriculture and writing.

In Egypt, as in Sumer, we see the feminine divine being associated with wisdom, in the form of the Egyptian goddess of truth and cosmic harmony Ma'at, whose name means 'truth'. The primary symbol of Ma'at was the feather, which she was depicted wearing on her head. Through Ma'at's feather we see wisdom being linked with airy concepts at a very early time, a syncretisation which would also be expressed very clearly later with the Shekinah.

These two great civilizations of ancient Egypt and Sumer with her successors significantly influenced the development of the Canaanites, who occupied the area which is roughly Israel, Lebanon and Palestine, as well as parts of the surrounding areas, today. As these civilizations influenced Canaan, so too did qualities of their gods become expressed as part of the Canaanite pantheon. The attributes of their mother goddess Asherah became conflated with some of the characteristics previously associated with both the Sumerian goddess Inanna and the Egyptian goddess Isis-Ma'at.

However we should also keep in mind that cross-fertilization is usually a two-way process. The Canaanite goddess Asherah was also imported back to Egypt and linked with the erotic Egyptian goddess Qudshu, as well as with the Syrian love and war goddess Astarte. From here other manifestations of the feminine divine would also occur, with the Syrian goddess Astarte giving rise to the Cyprian love goddess Aphrodite.

From the land of Canaan sprang the Semitic tribes who would subsequently become known as the Hebrews.[37] The Hebrews were exposed to the Babylonian and Egyptian myths, philosophies and ideas during the periods of exile/residence they experienced in these two ancient civilizations.

There are disputes over the historical accuracy of the Biblical description of Jewish slavery in Egypt described in *Exodus*. Historically however we know that there was a

---

37 Canaanites, Tubbs, 1999.

40

Jewish presence in Egypt after large numbers of Jews settled there for a time following the destruction of Judah in 597 BCE.

The evidence also indicates that a large group of Jews went into exile in Babylon following the destruction of Judah in 597 BCE. Many of these 'Babylonian' Jews returned to Judah in the period around 520-515 BCE to rebuild the Second Temple in Jerusalem.

The significance of the goddess Asherah to the early Hebrew tribes is clearly illustrated in the fact that forty references to her remain in the *Old Testament*. These references remain in the *Old Testament* books despite numerous changes to the writings as monotheism took over as the dominant religious style and the goddess Asherah was otherwise excised from religious practices. The divine feminine was however too important to be fully banished, and she soon re-emerged as the unnamed Wisdom Goddess.

The Wisdom Goddess drew on precedents from other cultures the Hebrews had been exposed to, *"seeing wisdom as an Israelite reflection or borrowing of a foreign mythical deity — perhaps Ishtar, Astarte, or Isis."*[38] Following the period where the Wisdom Goddess occurred in texts, around the third century BCE to the second century CE, camer the naming of wisdom as the Shekinah in the first-second century CE *Onkelos Targum.*

Contemporary with the Shekinah and drawing on some of the same earlier sources we see the Gnostic wisdom goddess, Sophia. There are many parallels between these two goddesses which suggest cross-fertilisation of ideas, which we will explore in more detail in subsequent chapters. It seems apparent that both the Shekinah and Sophia influenced perceptions of the Christian Holy Spirit and the Virgin Mary, seen in textual references to titles and motifs. The Islamic figure of Sakina is clearly derived from

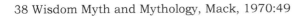

---

38 Wisdom Myth and Mythology, Mack, 1970:49

41

the Shekinah, both through her name and also the references to her in the *Qur'an*, as we will demonstrate.

Ancient textual evidence does not link the Sumerian goddess Lilith to the Shekinah. However allegorical references made in medieval Kabbalistic texts have encouraged us to consider the changing cultural perceptions of Lilith from Sumerian myths through to medieval Jewish tales to determine the extent of her influence on the portrayal of divine feminine wisdom.

Further afield, although there is no evidence that they are related, we see interesting parallels between the cultural manifestations of the divine feminine as the Shekinah and as the goddess Hekate in the *Chaldean Oracles* and the all-encompassing Indian goddess Shakti. It is a rich field and we need to explore all these avenues to appreciate the depth, significance and impact of the Shekinah in her development, and the patterns of influence and power which recur with the feminine divine.

The richest source of information about the Shekinah is the medieval Kabbalah, where she is sometimes known as the Greater Shekinah, the divine fire which surrounds and embraces God in a union which creates the universe, the angels and all the souls. She is also known as the Lesser Shekinah, in her role as the anima mundi (world soul). The roots of the idea that the soul of the Earth is an expression of the feminine divine may be found in the writings of the ancient Greek philosopher Plato (428-348 BCE) in his work *Timaeus* written in the fourth century BCE. Prior to this the earth and the universe itself were described as being made from the body of the goddess Tiamat in the Babylonian myths.

In the medieval Kabbalah this idea is taken a step further, with the Shekinah being directly equated to the world: *"God is the space of the world. What is the world? The Shekinah."*[39] In the Kabbalah, the material world is known as Malkuth (*'the Kingdom'*), the realm where we exist

---

39 Zohar IV:242a, C13th CE.

and where the four elements of air, earth, fire and water unite in different proportions to give physical form to everything. The elements are more than simply physical manifestations of energy states like solid, liquid and gas which form the building blocks of nature; they are also philosophical concepts and spiritual essences whose combinations engender the diversity of life.

Like the idea of the world soul, the elements also find their origins in ancient Greece, in the doctrines of the fifth century BCE Greek philosopher and root-magician Empedocles (490-430 BCE).[40] In his work *Tetrasomia* (*'Doctrine of Four Elements'*), Empedocles equated the four elements of air, fire, water and earth to gods and goddesses, and postulated that the two universal forces which caused all things to be attracted or dispersed were love and strife. According to Empedocles, love, the power of the love goddess Aphrodite, caused attraction, and strife, the power of the war god Ares, caused repulsion or dispersion.

This doctrine emphasises the way philosophies and deities cross-fertilised between cultures, with Aphrodite having her roots in the Syrian fertility and war goddess Astarte, who was equated to the Canaanite goddess Asherah. The interconnectedness of ideas and philosophies in the ancient world is something which must always be remembered when following the paths of assimilation, syncretisation and fusion which characterised so many of the deities of the age.

Whilst the exact origins of the Kabbalah are unknown, it is clear that cultural influences from ancient Greece, Egypt and Sumer/Babylonia played a key part in the development of its philosophies. According to legend, the Kabbalah was taught to Adam in the Garden of Eden by the archangel Raziel, who is predominantly associated with wisdom.

The term Kabbalah was first recorded in the teachings of the Jewish Rabbi Isaac the Blind (1160-1236 CE), in

---

40 Tetrasomia, Empedocles, C5th BCE.

Provence, France, who was known as the *'Father of Kabbalah'*. The main Kabbalistic texts and teachings stem from the tenth-twelfth century CE onwards, however one of the most important source texts used by Kabbalists, the *Sepher Yetzirah* (*'Book of Formation'*), dates back to the second century CE thereby suggesting earlier origins. Moreover many of the other philosophies and cosmologies which influenced the Kabbalah and its development, such as Gnosticism and Neo-Platonism, also date back to this earlier period.

The Kabbalah is essentially a philosophy and cosmology which explains human life and the universe through the ordering of chaos expressed as manifestations of the creative divine impulse at different levels. The process of manifestation subsequently produces matter and the creation of life. The central glyph of the Kabbalah is the Tree of Life, an ordered collection of ten circles (called *Sephiroth*, meaning *'emanations'*) connected by twenty-two paths, which symbolise man, the universe, and the process of creation.

The Shekinah can be found throughout Kabbalistic philosophies and the glyph of the Kabbalistic Tree of Life. Not only is the Shekinah specifically represented by two of the ten Sephiroth and connected with the process of creation through the Four Worlds which comprise the Kabbalistic Tree of Life, but she is also viewed as being the *Neshamah* or higher soul, which is a significant part of Kabbalistic philosophy. Additionally, the Shekinah is the feminine divine who is in a dynamic polarity with the masculine divine, resulting in creation and change. As such, she is both the Greater Shekinah who unites with God, and the Lesser or Exiled Shekinah who is the soul of the earth itself.

This relationship between the Shekinah and the Earth as anima mundi (world soul) has found a modern scientific outlet in the Gaia Hypothesis of the scientist James Lovelock, which argues that the Earth is a single self-regulating system which responds to changing circumstances. Whilst the scientists have not yet gone as far as to include a spiritual dimension in their idea that the Earth behaves as a single organism with the multitude of life and landscapes acting as a body, this does show how science and spirituality are drawing closer with time. From here it is one small step towards the perception that the anima mundi should exist, and should be feminine as she engenders creation. This is a perception presaged in the medieval Kabbalistic work, the *Bahir*, *"it is impossible for the lower world to endure without the female."*[41]

In Jewish tales the Shekinah ascends to heaven and descends to earth on different occasions. Originally there was no clear distinction between the Heavenly Shekinah and Earthly Shekinah, until Adam and Eve left Eden. Here then we may see the Heavenly Shekinah as representing the purity and innocence of Eden, the idealised Golden Age. She remained behind on earth but ascended through the seven heavens as a result of man's sins until she was reunited with God. The holiness of various prophets brought her back to dwell in the Temple of Solomon. The destruction of the Temple again saw her leave the Earth to ascend the heavens. The Temple of Solomon has come to represent an ideal, a place of wisdom, knowledge, skill and fellowship. This was described eloquently by the esoteric mason Frederick Holland in the 1880s, when he wrote on the Shekinah and said:

> *"In that temple, which is now in ruins, we pointed out the bush which was on fire and yet was not consumed; it was the glory of the Shekinah, it was the circle squared, but now it is destroyed and the cube circulated; the Shekinah has left it, the seven-coloured candle is seen no more, the twelve loaves are gone from the table, and the columns upon which the Temple rested are thrown down."*[42]

---

41 Bahir, 173, C12th CE.
42 The Revelation of the Shechinah, Holland, 1887.

Amongst the symbolism in these words is a reference to the seven archangels who are said to dwell in the presence of God, and by implication also the presence of the Heavenly Shekinah. These archangels include Gabriel, Michael, Raphael, and Uriel, all of whom are particularly associated with the Shekinah, being those who are said to preside over her four camps in heaven. The Shekinah is also often juxtaposed with the order of angels known as the Cherubim, who appear significantly as the guardians of Eden, were depicted on the Ark of the Covenant, and were also seen in Ezekiel's vision (in the *Book of Ezekiel*, sixth century BCE) which formed the basis for Merkavah mysticism.

It was in the Kabbalistic doctrines of the tenth century CE onwards that the Shekinah began to be more openly revealed as the divine feminine power opposite the masculine Yahweh. German Kabbalists in the tenth century expressed the doctrine that the Greater Shekinah encircled God as a circle of flame, and their union created not only the universe and the divine throne (as described in the *Book of Ezekiel*), but also the angels and human souls.[43]

The Heavenly Shekinah was seen as the divine bride, united with the masculine God in an equal relationship. This pattern was also repeated with the Earthly Shekinah being seen as the bride of the Sun/Son. The Heavenly Shekinah was viewed as the Mother and Yahweh as the Father, with the Lesser Shekinah being the Earth and divine Daughter, and the Sun (the Sephira of Tiphereth on the Qabalistic Tree of Life) being the divine Son. This mother-father relationship repeated the pattern of *'Yahweh and His Asherah'* found in the Hebrew tribes prior to the reforms of the seventh-sixth century BCE described in the *Old Testament Book of Deuteronomy*, which is discussed in more depth in the later chapter, *From Canaan*.

───────────────

43 Kabbalah, Ponce, 1974:64-67.

An old Kabbalistic commentary on *Genesis* noted, *"As His Shekinah is above, so is His Shekinah below."*[44] This was obviously influenced by the famous phrase *"As above, so below"* from the Emerald Tablet of alchemy, but is also relevant in its own right as an expression of the relationship between the Heavenly Shekinah and the Earthly Shekinah. The influence of the Sumerian wisdom goddess Inanna might also be felt here, with one of her greatest exploits, the descent into the underworld, being named *"From the great above to the great below."*

The depiction of the divine family is one of the key expressions of the greatest word of power, the Unpronounceable Name of God, or Tetragrammaton. This fourfold name is comprised of the Hebrew letters Yod, Heh, Vav, Heh corresponding respectively to the Father, Mother, Son, and Daughter. The correct pronunciation of Tetragrammaton, which was said to be immensely powerful and capable of destroying the universe, has been lost for centuries. Significantly, if the Yod, symbolising God the Father, is removed from this name, we are left with Heh Vav Heh, which spells Eve, the first woman of the *Book of Genesis* and some of the Gnostic texts.

The famous Kabbalist Rabbi Eleazer of Worms (1176-1238 CE), who was one of the first great propagators of the Kabbalah, said of the Earthly Shekinah that:

> *"The Shekinah is called the daughter of the creator ... and she is also called the tenth Sephira and royalty (Malkuth), because the crown of the kingdom is on his head."*[45]

As already discussed, the Shekinah is sometimes equated to the original paradise of Eden, and when in the Old Testament *Book of Deuteronomy*, we see the question, *"Is a tree in the field then a man who will come against*

---

44 Sepher Raziel, fol.36a, C13th CE.
45 Sepher ha-Hokhmah, C13th CE.

*you*",[46] it can be seen as referring to both the Kabbalistic Tree of Life as a macrocosmic symbol of the miniature universe within the human body, and also the Earthly Shekinah as the sum of all the trees, for she is known as *"the Field of Holy Apples"*.[47] This is why the practice of Kabbalah is also known as *'ascending to the orchard'*, referring to the desire to reclaim perfection internally in the self and externally in the world.

Indeed one of the most powerful and influential pieces of Kabbalistic writing is called *'Four Entered the Orchard'*, and refers to the attempt of four Rabbis to enter the throne room of God. Only one is successful, and their journey through the seven palaces forms the basis of Merkavah mysticism, a form of mysticism which seeks to reach the presence of God as described in the *Book of Ezekiel* and the apocryphal *Book of 3 Enoch*.

Another important and intriguing association with the Heavenly Shekinah is that of her healing light. The splendour of the Heavenly Shekinah was seen as a substance with miraculous powers, including protection from illness, demons and malice (*3 Enoch*), and also as a sustaining food for angels and saints. In this sense the Heavenly Shekinah is seen as the primordial emanation, the first light. This amazing light also links in to early interpretations of *Genesis* (*"Let there be Light"*),[48] and of Adam and Eve being clothed in a protective light before their fall. The interconnections between the Shekinah and different forms of light are discussed in the later chapter *Light of Creation*.

A significant reference connecting the Wisdom Goddess to light is found in the *Song of Solomon* in the verse, *"Who is this that looks forth like the dawn, fair as the moon, bright as the sun."*[49] We also see the emphasis on her light in the

---

46 Deuteronomy 20:19, C7th-C6th BCE.
47 Zohar 2:60b C13th CE.
48 Genesis 1:3, C10th-C8th BCE.
49 Song of Solomon 6:10, C3rd-C2nd BCE.

first century BCE wisdom text, *The Wisdom of Solomon*, where the Wisdom Goddess is described as *"the radiance that streams from everlasting light, the flawless mirror of the active power of God and the image of his goodness."*[50]

The Shekinah has also been identified by Kabbalists with the *Bath Kol*, or *'daughter of the voice'*, a term used to describe a heavenly voice which proclaimed God's will. Bath Kol occurs in both the *Old* and *New Testaments*, but was generally regarded as a manifestation which occurred following the decline of the great prophets. This is why Eleazer of Worms said of the Shekinah, *"She is called the king's daughter, sometimes she is also called, according to her mission daughter of the voice."*[51]

---

50 Wisdom of Solomon 7:26, C1st BCE, trans. Schäfer.
51 Sepher ha-Hokhmah, Eleazer of Worms, C12th CE.

# The Wisdom Goddesses : Timeline

(Overview)

| Time | Culture | Reference |
|---|---|---|
| C30th-20th BCE | Sumerian | Sumerian/Babylonian texts including mention of Inanna, Lilith and Siduri in myths |
| C28th-22nd BCE | Egyptian | Pyramid texts including Isis and Ma'at in spells |
| C20th-17th BCE | Egyptian | *Instruction to Merikara*, the first wisdom text, including reference to Ma'at |
| C15th-12th BCE | Canaanite | Ugaritic texts describing Asherah and Anat, and their connections to other deities in the pantheon |
| C8th-6th BCE | Hebrew | Pentateuch texts being written (J, E, P and D texts) including mentions of Asherah |
| C2nd-1st BCE | Hebrew | Wisdom texts describing the Wisdom Goddess, e.g. *Wisdom of Solomon, Jesus Sirach* |
| C2nd BCE – C4th CE | Gnostic | Wisdom Goddess in numerous texts as Edem, Sophia, Achamaoth, Barbelo |
| C1st BCE – C2nd CE | Greek | Hellenic writers describe Isis as saviour goddess in numerous texts |
| C1st-3rd CE | Jewish | *Onkelos Targum* first names the Shekinah |
| C2nd CE | Roman | *Chaldean Oracles* with cosmic Hekate |
| C3rd-9th CE | Jewish | Merkavah texts including reference to the Shekinah |
| C7th CE | Islamic | The *Quran* including reference to the Sakina |
| C12th-16th CE | Jewish | Kabbalistic texts including numerous references to the Shekinah |

# Part 2

# Aeons of Wisdom

# Shekinah Genesis

It is a simple truth that no religion springs forth fully formed, but rather that it draws from its antecedents, and continues to evolve. In order to study the Shekinah, we need to gain an awareness of her origins and to appreciate her place within it, we also need to understand that Judaism did not start out as a fully-formed monotheistic religion. Likewise there are numerous feminine divinities whose origins are conflated and entangled with that of the Shekinah, as well as many who have influenced her or who were influenced by her. In the following chapters we will explore the similarities, possible origins and other connections between the Shekinah and other relevant goddesses in ancient civilisations of the Middle East, including those of ancient Egypt, Sumer, Canaan and the Semitic tribes.

Before we look at earlier civilizations and their possible influences on the development of Jewish portrayals of divine feminine wisdom, we need to first investigate the formative process which led to the creation of the *Torah*. The documents which form the five books of the *Torah* may have been first compiled together between the seventh and fifth centuries BCE.[52] In the Documentary Hypothesis of Julius Wellhausen (1844-1918), these different fragments

---

52 Did God Have a Wife?, Dever, 2005:64-68.

which formed the *Torah* were known collectively as the J, P, E and D documents. Even with revisions following their collation, these books still retained traces of their polytheistic roots, which assist us in our quest for the divine feminine wisdom.

| Document | Period | Comprising |
|---|---|---|
| J ("Jahweh") | C10th-C8th BCE | Genesis<br>Exodus (first half)<br>Numbers (fragments) |
| E ("Elohim") | C9th-C8th BCE | Genesis (parts)<br>Exodus (parts) |
| D ("Deuteronomistic") | C7th-C6th BCE | Deuteronomy (and the other 7 Books through to 2 Kings) |
| P ("Priestly") | C6th-C5th BCE | Leviticus<br>Reworked texts of Genesis to Numbers |

In the ancient world the dissemination of the texts of the *Old Testament* to the Jews spread across numerous countries was a process which took centuries. For example, the Elephantine Jews (in Egypt) were ignorant of the biblical texts and their contents in the fifth century BCE, as evidenced by the *Passover Papyrus* (419 BCE)[53] and their worship of the goddess Anatyahu (Anat combined with a derivative of the name of Yahweh).

Furthermore, due to the minimal numbers of literate people with access to the *Old Testament* writings, *"this anthology was able to function as authoritatively religious literature only from, at the earliest, the time of Jesus Ben*

---

53 Ancient Aramaic and Hebrew Letters, Lindenberger, 2003:62.

*Sira, circa 200 BCE".*[54] Indeed, Eugene Ulrich stresses that *"there was no Bible in any meaningful sense until after the fall of Jerusalem to the Romans in 70 CE".*[55]

---

54 Was there Doctrinal Dissemination in Early Yahweh Religion, Noll, 2008:420.
55 Our Sharper Focus on the Bible and Theology Thanks to the Dead Sea Scrolls, Ulrich, 2004:1-24.

# From Canaan

*"Asherah has made a covenant with us."*
*~ Inscription from Arslan Tash, C7th BCE*

The developing kingdoms of Israel and Judah came to dominate the land of Canaan, a culture in decline, and in so doing they assimilated deities and practices as peoples and cultures intermingled. In this chapter we will examine the indispensable contributions made by Asherah and the Canaanite gods, including Yahweh, to the development of the Shekinah and indeed biblical literature as a whole. The Canaanite goddess Asherah is found throughout the *Old Testament*, and exhibits many key characteristics which suggest that she was one of the significant influences on the later Shekinah.

Accepting that the *Old Testament* did not originate from the pen of a single person, but rather was constructed from several different sources over a period of centuries, we can also see from the evidence that the God written about in the *Old Testament* was himself a composite deity. The different divine names found in the biblical books, including Yahweh, Elion and Elohim, initially referred to different gods from the Canaanite pantheon that subsequently became merged into the one god of the Hebrews. Part of this process was the discarding of Yahweh's divine wife, Asherah, which gained momentum around the seventh to sixth century BCE in the period that the *Book of*

*Deuteronomy* was written, hence *Deuteronomy 16:21* says *"Do not plant for yourself an Asherah, or any other tree near the altar that you will make yourselves for God [Yahweh] your Lord."*

The monotheistic reforms aimed at excising all other deities, particularly Asherah, are referred to in the seventh century BCE *Book of 2 Kings*, and were attributed to King Hezekiah (reigned 715-687/6 BCE) with the encouragement of the prophet Isaiah. They include cutting down the Asherah trees or poles, tearing down the *massēbôt* or standing stones, removing the high places or *bāmôt* where incense was burned to other deities, especially Asherah, and breaking up the bronze serpent called Neshushtan used for burning incense:

> *"He removed the high places, broke down the pillars, and cut down the sacred pole. He broke in pieces the bronze serpent that Moses had made, for until those days the people of Israel had made offerings to it; it was called Neshushtan."*[56]

In *2 Kings 23:7* we see a reference to *"where the women did weaving for Asherah"*, which might suggest the dressing of statues, another practice which was excised with the worship of other gods. The attempts to remove other deities took time, and this is reflected in similar references being made decades later in the *Book of Ezekiel* in the sixth century BCE:

> *"I will destroy your high places. Your altars shall become desolate, and your incense-stands shall be broken; and I will throw down your slain in front of your idols."*[57]

---

56 2 Kings 18:4-5, C7th BCE.
57 Ezekiel 6:3-4, C6th BCE.

Despite the eventual removal of the worship of Asherah from the Hebrew tribes, she was not viewed or treated as harshly as other gods. This is seen in the *Book of 1 Kings 18*, where the four hundred and fifty prophets of Baal were  slain by the prophet Elijah and his followers,[58] but the four hundred prophets of Asherah were spared. The fact that forty references to Asherah remained in the *Old Testament*[59] also indicates a reluctance to completely remove the goddess who had been the consort of Yahweh, the God of the *Old Testament*. As Olyan (1988:33) notes:

> *"(The goddess Asherah) was an acceptable and legitimate part of Yahweh's cult in non-deuteronomistic circles. The association of the Asherah and the cult of Yahweh suggests in turn that Asherah was the consort of Yahweh in circles both in the north and the south."*[60]

So where did Asherah and the gods of the Bible come from? Asherah is found in Ugaritic[61] texts from the  fourteenth-thirteenth century BCE as a Canaanite goddess as *"Lady Asherah of the Sea"*, with her name being

---

58 1 Kings 18:40, C7th BCE.
59 The forty references to Asherah, and the plural Asherim ('sacred poles') may be found in Exodus 34:13; Deuteronomy 7:5, Deuteronomy 12:3, Deuteronomy 16:21; Judges 3:7, Judges 6:25, Judges 6:26, Judges 6:28, Judges 6:30; 1 Kings 14:15, 1 Kings 14:23, 1 Kings 15:13, 1 Kings 16:32, 1 Kings 18:19; 2 Kings 13:6, 2 Kings 17:10, 2 Kings 17:16, 2 Kings 18:4, 2 Kings 21:3, 2 Kings 21:7, 2 Kings 23:4, 2 Kings 23:6, 2 Kings 23:7, 2 Kings 23:14, 2 Kings 23:15; 2 Chronicles 14:3, 2 Chronicles 15:16, 2 Chronicles 17:6, 2 Chronicles 19:3, 2 Chronicles 24:18, 2 Chronicles 31:1, 2 Chronicles 33:3, 2 Chronicles 33:19, 2 Chronicles 34:3, 2 Chronicles 34:4, 2 Chronicles 34:7; Isaiah 17:8, Isaiah 27:9; Jeremiah 17:2; Micah 5:14.
60 Asherah and the Cult of Yahweh in Israel, Olyan, 1988:33.
61 Ugarit was a city based on the modern Syrian coast, which was initially governed by Egypt, and whose texts were recorded in Akkadian, Hurritic, Sumerian and Ugaritic (an alphabetic cuneiform script).

translated as *"She Who Treads/Subdues Sea"*. She is identified as the mother of the gods and consort of El, the principal god of the pantheon, whose name would become one of those attributed to Yahweh. This is actually recorded in *Exodus*, where Yahweh is effectively assimilating El and showing that the earlier Patriarchs had worshipped the Canaanite god (and therefore logically his consort Asherah as well):

> *"I revealed Myself to Abraham, Isaac and Jacob as El Shaddai, and did not allow them to know Me by My name Yahweh. I also made my Covenant with them, promising to give them the land of Canaan, the land of their pilgrimage."*[62]

The name Canaan is a Hebrew word for the land (and its people) which encompassed Israel, Palestine, Lebanon, and parts of Jordan, Syria and northeast Egypt. The Canaanites may be traced back to roots in the Neolithic around 8500-8000 BCE.[63] Canaan occupied a crossroads position, with easy access to the major civilizations of Egypt and Mesopotamia (Sumer), and the Aegean Sea from its coastline, hence also to the Minoans on the island of Crete.

A clear indication of the roles of El and Asherah as the origins of the later biblical Yahweh and Shekinah is seen in the role of the Tent of Meeting as a divine enclosure. *Exodus* chapters 26-28 give detailed descriptions of the construction of the Tent of Meeting, which was also called the Tabernacle. The Tent of Meeting was the portable place of worship for Yahweh, and the Shekinah the divine presence which manifested there.

In an earlier Ugaritic text we see, *"They entered the tent of El and went into the tent-shrine of the King, the Father of Years."*[64] Indeed, the other Canaanite gods were also said to

---

62 Exodus 6:2-3, C10th-C8th BCE.
63 Canaanites, Tubb, 1998.
64 The Tent of El and the Israelite Tent of Meeting, Clifford, 1971:222.

live in tents, *"The gods go to their tents, the circle of El to their tabernacles."*[65] Significantly, *"Besides being a dwelling, the tent of El is a place of authoritative decree or oracle."*[66]

It is worth noting here that Asherah was sometimes known as Elath (or Elat), which simply means 'the Goddess'.[67] An example of this is seen in the seventh century BCE incantation text from Arslan Tash which reads *"Elat the Eternal One has made a covenant with us, Asherah has made a covenant with us."*[68]

Asherah is called Athirat ('aṯrt) in the Ugaritic texts,[69] which may mean *'sanctuary'* or *'holy place'*, and with this name she was known as the *'mother of the gods'*. These possible meanings would obviously fit perfectly with the nature of the Shekinah as the indwelling presence in the holy place. This is emphasised further by one of the Ugaritic myths, where after the god Baal had defeated the god Yam of the chaos waters he wanted a house (palace/temple) of his own. The goddess Anat importuned the god El to no avail, and it was only when Athirat interceded on Baal's behalf that he was granted his own house (KTU 1.3-1.4):

> *"Let a house be built for Baal like the gods, and a dwelling like the sons of Athirat! And the Great Lady-who-tramples-Yam (Asherah/ Athirat) replied: You are great, O El! The greyness of your beard does indeed make you wise."*[70]

---

65 The Tent of El and the Israelite Tent of Meeting, Clifford, 1971:223.

66 The Tent of El and the Israelite Tent of Meeting, Clifford, 1971:223.

67 The Goddess Asherah, Patai, 1965.

68 Yahweh and the God of the Patriarchs, Cross, 1962:237.

69 A Reconsideration of the Aphrodite-Ashtart Syncretism, Budin, 2004.

70 Religious Texts From Ugarit, Wyatt, 2002:101

An association of Athirat (Asherah) which is subsequently found with the Shekinah is that of breath. Indeed this connection could be viewed as forming another link in the attribution chain from the breath of Ma'at to the breath of the Shekinah. In an Ugaritic exorcism of a possessed adolescent (KTU 1.169), we see the significant lines:

> *"From delirium restored, lo, by the breath of Athirat the Great Lady in the heart may you be moulded."*[71]

Another significant reference in these texts is to the *seventy sons of Athirat'*, which was clearly the precursor to the later Jewish idea of the seventy guardian angels of the nations, found in texts like the *Book of Enoch* and implied in the symbolism of the branches of the menorah (sevenfold candlestick). It has been suggested that the common interpretation of the *Song of Solomon* of God and Israel as bride and groom is actually a gloss over its earlier depiction of the divine love of El and Asherah.[72] This would certainly be in keeping stylistically with much of the contemporary Mesopotamian, Egyptian and Ugaritic love poetry.

Asherah's name occurs forty times in the Bible, where it is commonly used to refer to her symbol of a carved wooden pole or tree, *"They set up for themselves pillars and Asherim (sacred poles) on every high hill and under every green tree; there they made offerings on all the high places."*[73] This carved wooden pole or tree was also known as a tree of life, and may be the antecedent of the Wisdom Goddess reference in *Proverbs 3:18*, *"She is a tree of life to those who lay hold of her"*.

The Greek translators of the *Old Testament* (often called the Septuagint) in the third-second century BCE took

---

71 Religious Texts From Ugarit, Wyatt, 2002:449.
72 Women in Ugarit and Israel: Their Social and Religious Position in the Context if the Ancient Near East, Marsman, 2003:703.
73 2 Kings 17:10-11, C7th BCE.

the Hebrew word *asherah* and used the Greek terms *'alsos* (*'grove'*) and *dendron* (*'tree'*) in its place. Later Latin translators working on the Vulgate Bible in the fourth century CE used the words *lucus* (*'copse'* or *'sacred grove'*) or *nemus* (*'forest'*) to replace *asherah*.[74]

As an aside, although there is no evidence to suggest a direct connection to these biblical translations, this use of the word grove also recalls the Celtic goddess Nemetona, whose name means *'Goddess of the sacred grove'*. Nemetona was worshipped around Bath in Somerset (England) during the period of the second-fifth century CE. Her worship however predates this by at least several centuries, with evidence for her worship widespread all over the European Celtic world in both the names of places and that of tribes.

Jane Carter has argued convincingly that the Greek Spartan goddess Ortheia, who was subsumed into the maiden huntress goddess Artemis around the fifth century BCE, was originally derived from Asherah.[75] Her argument is based on a number of factors, including the hundreds of terracotta masks found at the temple of Ortheia, which are unique in such quantities to the whole of Greece.

The name Ortheia, meaning *'upright'* or *'standing'* is taken from the story of how a lost wooden cult statue was found amongst trees by two Spartan men who subsequently went mad. Carter makes the connection between this wooden statue, which would preside over rites, and the carved poles (*Asherim*) used in the worship of Asherah. All of these elements, like the masks and poles could have been brought by the Phoenicians from the Middle East to Greece, and this is a plausible possibility for the origins of Ortheia.

It has likewise been suggested that Asherah is derived from the Babylonian goddess Ašratum, a fact which is substantiated by their equation in the bilingual deity list in

---

74 Did God Have a Wife?, Dever, 2008:225.
75 The Masks of Ortheia, Carter, 1987.

Ugaritic text RS 20.24.[76] In fact Ašratum is also equated to Athirat (one of the names of Asherah) in this text.[77] Ašratum is mentioned in Cuneiform writings from around the nineteenth century BCE as being the consort of the god Amurru,[78] and is sometimes equated to the earlier Sumerian grain goddess Gubarra.[79]  Her titles include *'bride of the king of heaven'* (i.e. queen of heaven) and *'mistress of sexual vigour and rejoicing'*.  These titles are reminiscent of the Sumerian goddess Inanna, and the sexual vigour associated with the Semitic/Egyptian goddess Qudshu.

At Kuntillet 'Ajrûd, about 50km south of Kadesh Barnea in Israel, can be found a wall inscription in a shrine room *"To Yahweh (of) Teiman and to his Asherah"*, and a large storage jar with an inscription which ends *"I blessed you by Yahweh of Samaria and by his Asherah"*.[80] Even more significant was the presence at the same site of a seated figure of Asherah, bare-breasted and on a lion throne. Other sites nearby like Khirbet al-Qom have likewise yielded finds from the ninth century BCE with this inscription on, showing it was not an isolated occurrence. However figurines going back as early as the nineteenth century BCE have been identified as being Asherah, in a distinctive pose associated with her, standing facing forward, naked, with long hair.

Asherah was known as the lady of the serpent (*dāt batni*),[81] this recalls the images of the Egyptian goddess Qudshu to whom Asherah was equated, and likewise the images of the Minoan Serpent Goddess whose worship can

---

76 A Reconsideration of the Aphrodite-Ashtart Syncretism, Budin, 2004:99.
77 Religious Texts From Ugarit, Wyatt, 2002:361.
78 Asherah in the Hebrew Bible and Northwest Semitic Literature, Day, 1986, p386
79 Asherah: Goddesses in Ugarit, Israel and the Old Testament. Binger, 1997:48.
80 Did God Have a Wife?, Dever, 2005:162.
81 Canaanite Myth and Hebrew Epic, Cross, 1997:33

be dated to around the sixteenth century BCE. Considering the trade between Canaan and Minos it is not difficult to understand how a goddess could have been imported, become conflated with or at the very least cross-fertilized a local deity with similar characteristics.

Lions were also frequently associated with Asherah, she was often depicted standing on the back of a lion, or seated on a lion throne. This was common for a number of Middle Eastern goddesses of the time, including Inanna, Astarte and Qudshu. Indeed there is *"a mass of inscriptional evidence from the Levantine Iron Age showing that a frequent epithet of the goddess Asherah was 'the Lion Lady'."*[82]

Looking at the times presented by the Biblical and other contemporary sources we discover an interesting phenomenon associated with Asherha and the Temple in Jerusalem. A statue of Asherah was placed in the Temple in Jerusalem around 928 BCE by Rehoboam, son of Solomon, following several centuries of her worship by the Hebrew tribes. This statue was removed and returned to the Temple several times in the centuries until its destruction in 586 BCE. This means that a statue of Asherah was in the Temple of Solomon for 236 of the 342 years of its lifespan (more than two thirds) as the tide ebbed backwards and forwards between monotheism and polytheism. It is clear that the worship of Asherah was popular and not easy to dispel, as seen when Manasseh replaced the altars in the temple which his father Hezekiah had destroyed:

> *"The carved image of Asherah that he had made he set in the house of which the Lord said to David and to his son Solomon, 'In this house, and in Jerusalem, which I have chosen out of all the tribes of Israel, I will put my name forever".*[83]

---

82 Did God Have a Wife?, Dever, 2005:166.
83 2 Kings 21:7, C7th BCE.

| Time | Statue removed by | Statue returned by |
|---|---|---|
| 928-893 BCE | | Rehoboam |
| 893-825 BCE | Asa | |
| 825-725 BCE | | Joash |
| 725-698 BCE | Hezekiah | |
| 698-620 BCE | | Manasseh |
| 620-609 BCE | Josiah | |
| 609-586 BCE | | Jehoahaz |

As well as statues there were also inscriptions of Yahweh and Asherah together. The earliest of these dates to around the eighth century BCE and was found in Jerusalem, and is the earliest known image of the god Yahweh, dating to the period when he was part of a pantheon rather than the sole god of the post-Deuteronomic-Jews.[84] As with other images of Yahweh, his gender is not emphasised and he is depicted without genitalia, and in this instant it is a simple figure with the face being an inverted triangle and stick-like legs.[85] Thus we can see that Asherah was the first divine wife of Yahweh, replaced by the Wisdom Goddess, and then at a later date by the Shekinah as the bride of Yahweh.

Significantly the Kabbalistic text, the *Zohar* makes the connection between Asherah and the Shekinah, when it says, *"The truth is that the Heh is called Asherah, after the name of its spouse, Asher."*[86] Asher can mean *'blessedness'*, *'happiness'*, *'good luck'*, or *'in order that'*, and here it is being used in the context of the divine name given to the highest aspect of God - *Eheieh Asher Eheieh* (*'I am that I am'*). Heh here refers to the letter attributed to the Heavenly Shekinah and Earthly Shekinah in the Tetragrammaton or Unpronounceable Name of God.

---

84 An Iron Age II Pictorial Inscription from Jerusalem Illustrating Yahweh and Asherah, Gilmour, 2009:87-103.
85 An Iron Age II Pictorial Inscription from Jerusalem Illustrating Yahweh and Asherah, Gilmour, 2009:99-100.
86 Zohar I.49a, C13rd CE.

In summary, it is clear that Asherah was an extremely important goddess to the cultures of both the Canaanites and the Hebrews. Moreover, Yahweh, the god of the Hebrews, came from the god of the same name worshipped previously by the Canaanites. To make the move to monotheism, the Hebrews outlawed practices and beliefs associated with Asherah and other deities. This process of transformation to the recognisable form defined by the *Old Testament* and contemporary literary works took several centuries to achieve. It required several more centuries to spread the new standard of *'worship from the book'* to the various Jewish communities spread throughout the ancient world.

Bearing these factors in mind, it seems clear that the Wisdom Goddess described in biblical texts such as *Proverbs* and wisdom literature such as *Jesus Sirach* and the *Wisdom of Solomon* was a survival of the goddess Asherah in an unnamed, and thus acceptable, form. Other cultural influences such as the Egyptians and Babylonians must now be considered to further explore the process whereby the unnamed Wisdom Goddess was named and acknowledged as the Shekinah.

# From Egypt

Echoes of the religion, culture and technological advances of the Ancient Egyptians can still be found throughout the world today. Many Jews settled in parts of Egypt following the destruction of the Kingdom of Judah by the Assyrians in 537 BCE, and would have been subject to the influences of Egyptian philosophy, cosmology and culture.

Bearing this in mind, when we turn to Ancient Egypt for clues about the origins of the Shekinah, it is unsurprising that we find Egyptian goddesses who may have connections to her, in particular Qudshu and Ma'at. Of course the goddess Isis should also be given due consideration as her cult assimilated the qualities and myths of numerous other goddesses, including Ma'at, and most certainly had an influence on the development of the Wisdom Goddess, and likely that of the Gnostic Sophia.

## Qudshu

There are sixteen or so Egyptian plaques from the New Kingdom (sixteenth-eleventh century BCE) showing Qudshu (who is also called Qadesh),[87] a naked goddess facing forward standing on a lion, holding lotuses in her right hand and a serpent in her left hand. On one of these

---

87 The Religions of Israel, Zevit, 2003:323.

plaques the names Qudshu, Anat and Astarte are all given to the figure, equating these three goddesses, and providing us with a link in the history of the Shekinah. As Helck (1971:464) observed:

> *"The stela carrying the inscription 'Qudšu-Astarte-Anat' has given rise to widespread acceptance of Qudšu as an alternative name for Asherah since Asherah in the Ugaritic texts seems to be called qdš."*[88]

An example from the Ugaritic texts which supports the equation of Qudshu to Asherah is the use of both the terms *'Sons of Asherah (Athirat)'* and *'Sons of Qudshu'*, to represent the gods.[89]

The name Qudshu means *'Holy One'* in ancient Egyptian and seems to be the name given to Asherah and/or Anat when she was assimilated into the Egyptian pantheon.[90]  Budin (2004:100) notes that *"no clear cognate for the goddess can be found in the Canaanite pantheons, and it appears that she emerged out of an amalgam of Ashtart and Anat in Egypt, thus becoming her own goddess."*[91] Qudshu is derived from the Semitic, and comes from the word Qadosh, meaning *'holy'* (and seen in words like Ruach HaQadosh, the *'spirit of holiness'* associated with prophecy and the Shekinah).  That she was not a native Egyptian goddess is made clear by her full frontal nakedness, which was never seen in any depictions of the indigenous Egyptian goddesses.

---

88 Die Beziehungen Agyptens zu Vorderasien im 3. und 2. Jahrtausend v.
Chr. 2, Helck, 1971:464 n.153.

89 Asherah: Goddesses in Ugarit, Israel and the Old Testament. Binger, 1997:58-63

90 The Queen Mother and the Cult in Ancient Israel, Ackerman, 1993:397.

91 A Reconsideration of the Aphrodite-Ashtart Syncretism, Budin, 2004:100

It is interesting to note that Qudshu was often linked with the Egyptian cow goddess Hathor due to similarities in their functions. In some of the pictures of Qudshu, she is depicted wearing what is known as a Hathor Wig, due to its particular association with images of the goddess Hathor. Hathor's name means 'house of Horus', referring to the Egyptian hawk-headed god Horus. The house reference reminds us of the way the Shekinah was viewed as the indwelling presence within the Temple of Solomon and the Ark of the Covenant.

As a goddess Qudshu was not worshipped in isolation, but rather was associated with the Egyptian phallic fertility god Min and the West Semitic war and thunder god Reshef as a triad. Like a number of other goddesses of the ancient world, Qudshu was sometimes shown standing on a lion, though in her case it was often between the two gods Min and Reshef on either side of her.

As part of her worship in the Near East, Qudshu and Reshef were the deities involved in a hieros gamos or sacred marriage by their worshippers,[92] recalling that of the Sumerian goddess Inanna and her consort the shepherd god Dumuzi, by the high priestess of Inanna and the king, though there is no evidence that this practice continued in Egypt.

A title often used for Qudshu was 'Lady of the Sky', which fits with the heavenly qualities often associated with wisdom. That she is depicted as holding serpents and lotuses demonstrates both her magical and erotic powers. Qudshu was linked with female sexuality, as a powerful force of fertility and magic, not a meek and passive sexuality. Amulets of Qudshu were used as apotropaic protections, and also for ensuring fertility.

The posture of Qudshu holding serpents is almost identical to the figure of the Minoan Serpent Goddess, who was worshipped on Crete around the sixteenth century

---

92 The Complete Gods & Goddesses of Ancient Egypt, Wilkinson, 2003:164.

BCE, making them contemporaries. However, whereas Qudshu was depicted as being completely naked, the Minoan goddess was shown bearing her breasts, but otherwise clothed. There is no known evidence to prove a direct descent of one from the other, nevertheless we can speculate, as other authors have,[93] that there may have been a cross-fertilization of ideas between the Egyptians and the mercantile sea-going Minoans, who were trading with each other at the time.

# Ma'at

The parallels between the Shekinah and the earlier ancient Egyptian goddess of natural balance, Ma'at, are quite striking. The goddess Ma'at was depicted as a (commonly winged) beautiful woman with a feather on her brow, which was her particular symbol, the feather of truth. Her name means *'truth'*, and she also represented wisdom, justice and the natural order of the universe.

Ma'at has ancient roots, stretching back into the dawn of Egyptian civilization. She is first mentioned in the earliest of all known Egyptian writings, the *Pyramid Texts*, which were engraved on the walls inside chambers in the pyramids from 2700-2200 BCE.

Ma'at was seen as either the daughter or wife of the sun and creator god Ra, a pairing that would be seen later with the Shekinah as the daughter or bride of Yahweh the creator god.

Viewed as the natural order of creation, Ma'at embodied the natural order which even the other Egyptian gods had to maintain, and this is why the hieroglyph for the plinth, on which all statues stood, was attributed to Ma'at as the underlying foundation.

---

93 E.g. Marinatos, 2000:112

The feather of truth emphasised her connection with air and breath, which can also be seen from such phrases as giving *'life to his nostrils'* with respect to Ra. This symbolism of the life-giving breath is another motif which recurs in the Shekinah imagery found in subsequent Jewish texts.

In light of her association with justice, and the fact that Egyptian judges wore an amulet of the feather of Ma'at as a sign of their rank, it is interesting to note the Shekinah would also subsequently be mentioned in connection with judges in the *Talmud* (*Berachot 6a*), *"when three sit as judges, the Shekhinah is with them."*

A striking image associated with Ma'at is *"the beautiful face of Ma'at shining from the heart of Ra"*.[94] The idea of the splendour of her face shining is also paralleled in descriptions of the glory shining from the face of the Heavenly Shekinah in later Jewish texts, including *3 Enoch.*

Another parallel between Ma'at and the Shekinah is to be found in the concept that Ma'at could be seen as a nourishing substance which sustained both the gods and men. Likewise the radiance of the Shekinah was said to sustain the angels and saints in *3 Enoch.*

Having demonstrated a number of parallels between Ma'at and the Shekinah, we need to turn to wisdom literature, which was amongst the most important texts of ancient Egypt, as an important part of Egyptian culture, for *"there does not exist one born wise"*.[95] Manuals of wisdom literature were taught to children and contained all the essentials for being a valued member of the community, including ethics and manners. This idea of virtuous behaviour equated to *'upholding Ma'at'*, and everyone in society, from the lowest peasant to the Pharaoh to the gods needed to uphold Ma'at to preserve order and harmony, and prevent chaos. The first of the known wisdom texts was the *Instruction to Merikara*, probably written between 2000-

---

94 Egyptian Mythology, Pinch, 2002:160
95 The Instruction of Ptahhotep, line 41, 2450 BCE.

1700 BCE. Karenga described this connection in her work on Ma'at (2004:60):

> "'Maat comes to him in its pure essence like the condition of the sayings of the ancestors' (Merikara, 34-35). Maat here is linked with two main elements, wisdom and tradition. Wisdom or knowledge, as argued below, is an ethical requirement. Here Maat is said to come to a wise person in its pure essence."[96]

The influence of Egyptian wisdom literature on the *Book of Proverbs* 1-9 has been argued by a number of scholars,[97] which then also suggests the influence of the goddess Ma'at on the unnamed Wisdom Goddess found in the *Book of Proverbs*, and subsequently in other Jewish wisdom literature such as *Jesus Sirach* and the *Wisdom of Solomon*. This influence would also make sense when Ma'at is considered as *"the personification of the order of the world which was established at the time of creation"*,[98] a role which is paralleled to an extent in the descriptions of the Wisdom Goddess and Sophia.

The upholding of Ma'at by all mankind and even the gods is paralleled in the subsequent relationship between man and the Shekinah. Thus in the *Kiddushin ('Betrothal')*, one of the tracts of the *Nashim ('Women')*, part of the *Talmud*, we see a clear indication of the relationship between personal behaviour and the nearness of the Earthly Shekinah:

> "He who commits a transgression, it is as if he pushes away the feet of the Shekinah."[99]

---

96 Maat: The Moral Ideal in Ancient Egypt, Karenga, 2004:60.
97 E.g. Bauer-Kayatz (1966), McKane (1970), Fontaine (1981).
98 Conceptions of God in Ancient Egypt, Hornung, 1996:74.
99 Kiddushin, 31a, in the Mishnah, C3rd CE.

Although she is not specifically connected to the Shekinah by direct association of image in ancient times, it seems likely that the concepts embodied by Ma'at were borrowed by the Hebrew tribes and incorporated into the Shekinah. Later evidence for this may be seen in the Merkavah text *Shiur Qoma*, where the Shekinah and truth (which is inherent to Ma'at) are connected, *"Truth is the place of the Shekinah who establishes all creatures in truth."*[100]

An even clearer and startling parallel to the ancient Egyptian cosmological weighing of the heart on the scales of Ma'at in the underworld is also seen in the *Shiur Qoma*:

> *"And scales of truth rest before him and the book of the account of the world are opened before him and he is a witness [Metatron] and makes known the deeds of everyone. And all thoughts of the heart are revealed to him, as it is said, 'I the Lord probe the heart, examine the kidneys and heart to repay each person according to his ways, like a fruit of his deeds'."*[101]

Another possible parallel on the theme of truth is seen in the alleged use of the name Aletheia (*'truth'* or *'disclosure'*) by the Gnostics. Both Iraneus and Hippolytus claim that the Gnostics worshipped Aletheia, however as they were both anti-Gnostic Christians and the term is not used in any extant Gnostic texts this must be regarded with suspicion.

Iraneus describes the duality of Pater (*'Father'*) and Aletheia (*'Truth'*) as part of the original Tetrad of four powers, and also that Ennoia (*'Thought'*) is part of the first duality in the same Tetrad, who birthed Aletheia. He also ascribes this theology to the Gnostic Valentinus, writing that:

---

100 Shiur Qoma, 2b:10-11, C7th-C12th CE.
101 Shiur Qoma, 2b:15-19, C7th-C12th CE.

*"And he declares that the Holy Spirit was produced by Aletheia for the inspection and fructification of the Aeons, by entering invisibly into them, and that, in this way, the Aeons brought forth the plants of truth."[102]*

# Isis

The influence of Isis on Wisdom Goddess literature is primarily from the Greco-Egyptian or Hellenic Isis. The Hellenic Isis' mythology, roles and functions assimilated not only that of Aset or Isa (the Egyptian names for Isis), but also that of other Egyptian goddesses such as Hathor, Ma'at and Sekhmet.

The Ptolemaic Greeks who ruled Egypt from 305-30 BCE adopted Isis as a major deity and her worship spread into Greek and Roman religions. The Egyptian Isis was originally a minor deity, whose cult quickly grew in importance in the Old Kingdom (2686-2181 BCE), as can be seen by the fact that, *"Isis above all is simply 'the divine one,' or 'great of divine-ness'."*[103]

The authors of works written around the time that the worship of Hellenic Isis was in the ascendancy (second-first century BCE) would have been aware of Hellenic and Egyptian ideas, and Kloppenborg (1982:58) points out the references to the earlier writings of Hesiod and Homer, as well as Egyptian religious practices, found in the first century BCE Jewish wisdom text, the *Wisdom of Solomon*.[104] Mack went further and demonstrated a likely line of descent for the Jewish wisdom literature, stating:

102 Against Heresies, Book 1, Iraneus, C2nd CE.
103 Conceptions of God in Ancient Egypt: The One and the Many, Hornung, 1996:63-4.
104 Isis and Sophia in the Book of Wisdom, Kloppenborg, 1982:58.

*"This derivation of wisdom mythology from the mythos of Isis can, moreover, be traced through Sirach and the Wisdom of Solomon to Philo of Alexandria."*[105]

As Mack observes, Isis *"during the Hellenistic period, becomes identified with Maat and in fact assumes Maat's cosmic functions."*[106] In light of this identification, there is an interesting parallel between Isis-Ma'at as the daughter/bride of the creator god Ra, and the Shekinah as the daughter/bride of Yahweh in Kabbalistic texts.

*"By identification with Maat, Isis takes over this function and adds soteirological motifs taken from her role in the myths of Horus and Osiris. The wisdom hymn in Proverbs 8:22, like the similar hymn in Sirach 24, reflects this general cosmic pattern of myth."*[107]

Indeed the aretalogical[108] pattern seen in the *Wisdom of Solomon* 6:22-10:21 mirrors earlier Isis aretalogies, as does the later Gnostic text *The Thunder, Perfect Mind.*[109] In addition to such aretalogical literature numerous significant writers in the ancient world promoted the view of Isis as multi-powered saviour, including the Greek geographer Artemidorus of Ephesus (*Geography*) and the Greek historian Diodorus Siculus (*Library of History*) in the first century BCE, the Greek historian and philosopher Plutarch (*On the Worship of Isis and Osiris*), the Berber writer and philosopher Apuleius (*Metamorphoses*, better known as *The*

---

105 Wisdom: Myth and Mytho-logy: Mack, 1970:54.
106 Ibid, 1970:54.
107 Ibid, 1970:54.
108 An aretalogy is a first person deity list of attributions in poem or hymn form.
109 Isis and Sophia in the Book of Wisdom, Kloppenborg, 1982:59-61.

*Golden Ass*) and the Egyptian priest Isidorus (*Hymns to Isis*) in the second century CE.

Of these texts the best known is probably Apuleius' *Metamorphoses*, with its inclusive Isis speech where she equates herself to numerous other goddesses including Ceres, Diana, Hekate, Juno, Minerva, Proserpina and Venus. What is particularly interesting about this speech is the list of powers and roles Isis ascribes to herself, which are very similar to those describing the Shekinah in subsequent Jewish writings, viz:

> *"I am she that is the natural mother of all things, mistress and governess of all the Elements, the initial progeny of worlds, chief of powers divine, Queen of heaven! the principal of the Gods celestial, the light of the goddesses: at my will the planets of the air, the wholesome winds of the Seas, and the silences of hell be disposed; my name, my divinity is adored throughout all the world in divers manners, in variable customs and in many names"*[110]

Another interesting motif seen in the Isis myths which also occurs in the Inanna and Asherah myths is that of the tree of life. In the case of Isis, this was both the sycamore tree, which was sacred to her, and also a form of her husband the vegetation god Osiris who was represented by the stylised djed pillar. The djed pillar symbolised the resting place of his body in a tree after his death and dismemberment at the hands of his brother, the chaos god Seth. A later variation of this symbolism can be seen in the human body being mapped onto the Kabbalistic Tree of Life.

The connection between Isis and the serpent (another wisdom motif) occurs in a number of ways. Isis used a serpent made from his own saliva to poison and trick the creator god Ra into revealing his true name to her and so

---

110 Metamorphoses Book 11.47, Apuleius, C2nd CE.

giving her his power, effectively elevating her to the status of the creator god.

Isis was often portrayed with the Uraeus serpent crown at her brow, which represented rulership and power, and also merged with the serpent goddess Renenutet, as well as the serpent goddess Hermouthis to form the serpentine Isis-Hermouthis, who probably influenced the Gnostic goddess Edem.

Looking at the Egyptian goddesses we have considered, it seems likely that Qudshu was derived in part or whole from Asherah, but did not figure in the development of the Wisdom Goddess or the Shekinah.

The goddess Ma'at however displays many characteristics and roles which are later found in both the Wisdom Goddess and the Shekinah, suggesting that Ma'at may have contributed to their development. Whether this was purely as Ma'at, or as Isis-Ma'at we cannot say, but the evidence is strongly supportive of a connection between her and the Wisdom Goddess and Shekinah.

The influence of Isis seems to have been more into the development of Sophia through her Greco-Egyptian form of Hellenic Isis. This is a theme which is explored further in the later chapter *Mother of Aeons*. Overall, it seems very likely that there was an Egyptian influence into the development of the subsequent wisdom goddesses. We shall next consider the possible influence on the Shekinah of the first known wisdom goddess, the ancient Sumerian wisdom goddess Inanna.

# From Ancient Sumer

The ancient Middle East was a melting pot of cultures, with a number of extremely influential civilizations and cultures rising and falling over the three millennia leading to the historical shift from BCE (Before the Christian Era) to CE (Christian Era). Amongst these the Sumerians, (whose civilization and culture would be replaced by the Babylonians, the Akkadians and the Assyrians) were a significant power, as were the later Semitic tribes who would assimilate some of their ideas and become the Hebrews.

The Sumerian goddess Inanna and her myths provide us with the first possible identifiable root for the Shekinah. Based on later attributions made in Jewish and Kabbalistic writings, we must also examine the early history of Inanna's contemporary, the goddess Lilith, who would become demonised and adopted into later cultures

## Inanna

A biblical reference to the *'queen of heaven'* gives us a clear indication of a possible earlier pre-Egyptian source for Asherah. The seventh century BCE *Book of Jeremiah* records his protests at the women's activities:

*"The children gather wood, the fathers kindle fire, and the women knead dough, to make cakes for the queen of heaven."[111]*

The Queen of Heaven was a name given to Astarte, Inanna and Ishtar (the Babylonian form of Inanna), and takes us to one of the first civilizations, that of the city states of Sumer. The tales of Inanna, Queen of Heaven, are the beginning of our journey searching for the Shekinah. Although the stories are believed to be at least a thousand years older than the foundation of the first city states, it is at the historical point of the creation of writing, around 3500 BCE, that we must begin. The first cities were built between 5000-4000 BCE, and what is commonly called Sumer was a collection of a dozen or so independent city-states, each with its own tutelary deity. Of these, the one which particularly concerns us is Uruk, the city of Inanna.

The story of *Inanna and the God of Wisdom* tells of how divine wisdom was transmitted to mankind. The goddess Inanna decided to visit her father (or grandfather depending on the version of the story) Enki, the god of wisdom. Enki greatly honoured Inanna, and toasted her many times, which caused him to get very drunk. As he got drunker he gave her more and more of the *me* with his toasts. The *me* were powers, the qualities which created civilization, from speech and truth to justice and crafts. Inanna gratefully received all of the *me* from him, and when Enki was settled in his drunken slumber she fled, knowing he would want them all back when he sobered up and realised what he had done. With the aid of her servant and friend Ninshibur, Inanna escaped all the creatures and traps Enki set for her and returned to her city of Uruk. There she gave the *me* to her people, and when Enki saw how they benefitted from them, he agreed that humanity should have the *me*.

---

111 Jeremiah 7:18, C7th BCE.

What is significant is that Inanna is the first deity who bestows wisdom on humanity, in the form of the *me*. So Inanna is the first goddess of wisdom, and she was also known as the Queen of Heaven.

A significant motif connection between Inanna, Asherah, the Wisdom Goddess and the Shekinah is that Inanna was linked to the tree of life, as the huluppu tree in her garden in the tale of *The Huluppu Tree*. From the emblems in the story it can be seen as the prototype of subsequent world tree stories.

In the story, Inanna plants the Huluppu (willow) tree in her garden, but a serpent nests in its roots, an Anzu bird (a lion-headed eagle) nests in the branches and the goddess Lilith nests in the trunk. This early appearance of Lilith in the tree is significant, and we will consider her shortly. The serpent (or dragon) in the roots and bird in the branches are motifs subsequently found in many world tree tales.

The hero Gilgamesh drives off the animals and chops the tree down at the behest of Inanna, so she can build a throne and bed from it. It is significant that in the tale Lilith is described as fleeing to the wild and uninhabited places, as this is where she was subsequently described as dwelling in later Jewish writings.

Gilgamesh also encountered a goddess called Siduri (*'young woman'*) who is called a goddess of wisdom (*nēmequ*) on his journey in the first great hero tale, *The Epic of Gilgamesh* (c. 2150-2100 BCE), who from the text appears to be a form of Inanna/Ishtar.[112] She advised him to live in the now rather than seek eternal life, with words which are extremely similar to the later (arguably derivative) biblical text of *Ecclesiastes*. Siduri told Gilgamesh:

> *"You will never find the life for which you are looking. When the gods created man they allotted to him death, but life they retained in their own keeping. As for you, Gilgamesh, fill*

112 Hymn to the Queen of Nippur, Lambert, 1982.

> *your belly with good things; day and night,*
> *night and day, dance and be merry, feast and*
> *rejoice. Let your clothes be fresh, bathe yourself*
> *in water, cherish the little child that holds your*
> *hand, and make your wife happy in your*
> *embrace; for this too is the lot of man."*[113]

In comparison, see the similar sentiments expressed in *Ecclesiastes* below. Note the reference to garments always being white, symbolising purity (and worn by the priesthood) in the ancient Egyptian world:

> *"Go, eat your bread with enjoyment, and drink*
> *your wine with a merry heart; for God has long*
> *ago approved what you do. Let your garments*
> *always be white; do not let oil be lacking on*
> *your head. Enjoy life with the wife whom you*
> *love, all the days of your vain life that are given*
> *you under the sun, because that is your portion*
> *in life and in your toil at which you toil under*
> *the sun."*[114]

Sumerian cylinder seal images from the third millennium BCE (around 2300-2200 BCE) show an unnamed horned goddess figure sitting with another figure on either side of a stylised tree of life, which has seven branches and a serpent on the trunk, recalling the story of the Huluppu Tree. This image is easy to translate into a biblical one, of the tree of knowledge with the serpent around the trunk, and might also be seen as a prototype for the menorah, the stylised seven branched candlestick of Judaism which can represent the Qabalistic Tree of Life.

Returning to the father of Inanna, the wisdom god Enki or Ea, recent research has contributed an interesting suggestion regarding his influence on the wisdom goddess of *Proverbs 8*. Lenzi (2006) points out that *Proverbs 8:22-31*

---

113 The Epic of Gilgamesh, C21st-C20th BCE.
114 Ecclesiastes 9:7-9, C4th-C2nd BCE.

is full of references to water, and that *"the disputed verb in Prov 8:23, sounds very much like a common epithet for Ea [Enki], the Mesopotamian god of water and wisdom, namely, naššīki (usually spelled niššīki), 'the prince.'"*[115] From this viewpoint Lenzi demonstrates the similarity between *Proverbs* 8:22-31 and the much earlier Babylonian *Enuma Elish* Tablet 1:79-108.[116] Here again we see an interesting earlier pairing of a creator god (Ea/Enki) with a wisdom goddess (Inanna), which is also seen subsequently in the relationship between Yahweh and both the Wisdom Goddess and also the Shekinah.

# Lilith

One of the most challenging and misunderstood female figures in history is the goddess Lilith. The first mention of Lilith is when she appears in the Sumerian tale of *The Huluppu Tree* some 5000 years or more ago.

Lilith's roots are believed to come from the Lilitu, the Sumerian winged wind and storm demons first mentioned around 3000 BCE. Other early sources which may have been assimilated into Lilith are the taloned Lil birds of Assyria and the Syrian demoness/goddess Lamashtu, known for preying on pregnant women and young children. Fröhlich (2010:102-3) details the connections between these different beings, as well as giving a description of Lilith. The leonine and serpentine connections are of particular note, when considering the frequency of their occurrence in the quest for the development of the Shekinah:

> *"The name Lilitu is to be identified here with that of Lilith as well as in the incantation texts*

115 Proverbs 8:22-31: Three Perspectives on Its Composition, Lenzi, 2006:700.
116 Proverbs 8:22-31: Three Perspectives on Its Composition, Lenzi, 2006:700-705.

*written against the demons of the lilû-family. Lilith is dangerous, above all for newborn babies, sucking their blood and eating their flesh. Her characteristics are very similar to those of the Mesopotamian female demon Lamaštu. She is represented on her numerous representations with lion head, female body, bird's legs, holding snakes in her hands, and suckling a dog and a swine."[117]*

The only biblical reference to Lilith is found in *Isaiah 34:14*, in which she was described as one of the spirits who would lay waste to the land on the day of vengeance:

*"Wildcats shall meet with hyenas, goat-demons shall call to each other; there too Lilith shall repose, and find a place to rest."[118]*

The best known story of Lilith is as the first woman who refused to lie under Adam during sexual congress and then flew off to the desert using the power of the Unpronounceable Name (the Tetragrammaton). Yahweh sent three angels called Semoy, Samsenoy and Semangelof after her, but they could not compel her return, and told her if she did not go back with them Yahweh would kill one hundred of her demon children every day. She agreed and said if the names of the three angels were placed on amulets they would serve as protection for newborn children from her vengeance. However this baby-killing Lilith is not an ancient figure, as this tale first occurs in the *Alphabet of Ben Sirra*, an eight-tenth century CE text. Lamashtu, however, did kill young children, and could be the source of this attribution to Lilith.

The negative qualities ascribed to Lilith as a baby-killer may also be directly derived from the qualities ascribed to

---

117 Theology and Demonology in Qumran Texts, Fröhlich, 2010:102-3.
118 Isaiah 34:14, C7th-C6th BCE.

the demon called Obizuth in the second century CE text the *Testament of Solomon*.[119]   This tale is one of the key foundations forming the basis for the later medieval and Renaissance grimoires for conjuring angels and demons. In the *Testament of Solomon*, King Solomon summoned many demons and learned of their powers and roles, and which angels could bind them, and he forced the demons to build the temple for him. Obizuth describes herself saying:

> *"I am called among men Obizuth; and by night I sleep not, but go my rounds over all the world, and visit women in childbirth. And divining the hour I take my stand; and if I am lucky, I strangle the child. But if not, I retire to another place. For I cannot for a single night retire unsuccessful."*[120]

The depiction of Lilith as a night-riding demon stealing men's nocturnal emissions is indicated by some of the Jewish amulets and magic bowls found at Nippur in Iraq. These date to around the fifth to sixth century CE and show the tradition of Lilith as a negative figure had already been established.

Interestingly a number of the amulets refer to male and female Liliths, indicating her name was being used for a type of demon who was believed to be able to shift gender. Thus we see:

> *"I adjure and command you, you all kinds of male and female demons, male and female Liliths, evil spirits, male and female harmers, those from the fire, and those from the water, and those from the wind, and those from the earth."*[121]

---

119 Testament of Solomon, 58, C2nd CE.
120 Testament of Solomon, 58, C2nd CE.
121 Dramatis Personae in the Jewish Magical Texts, Shaked, 2006. The essay contains numerous similar examples from this period.

The traditional Jewish view of Lilith is negative, and the *Talmud* describes Lilith as a female demon with a woman's face, wings and long hair.[122]   The long hair occurred in the earliest descriptions of Lilith and demonstrated her unmarried and hence sexually available status. This is alluded to in the *Testament of Solomon* when Solomon orders the hair of the demon Obizuth to be bound when she is hung in front of the Temple.[123]

Even in modern Qabalah Lilith is described negatively as the Qlipha of the Sephira (*'emanation'*) of Malkuth. Qlipha means *'shell'*, and is a term often incorrectly used to denote the so-called demonic being of a realm as evil.

The thirteenth century Kabbalistic treatise by Rabbi Isaac called *The Treatise on the Left Emanation* explored some of the more challenging aspects of the Kabbalistic theology and philosophies.  In this text Lilith was discussed in detail, and there were two Liliths described – a lesser Lilith and a greater Lilith.  This mirrors the Shekinah with her Heavenly and Earthly forms.  This mirroring is further seen in the greater Lilith being married to Samael the demon king.

Lilith was also described in *The Treatise on the Left Emanation* as Matron Lilith, recalling the attribution of the Shekinah as Matronit or Bride of the Sabbath:

> *"Both Samael and Lilith called Eve the Matron – also known as the Northern One – are emanated from beneath the Throne of Glory."*[124]

The lesser Lilith was married to Asmodeus the demon prince.  Samael and Lilith may be seen as both mirroring Adam and Eve, and also Yahweh and the Shekinah.

---

122 Eruvin 100b, Talmud, C3rd CE.
123 Testament of Solomon, 59, C2nd CE.
124 Treatise on the Left Emanation, Isaac Ben Jacob ha-Kohen, C13th CE.

The *Zohar* is explicit about there being a connection between Lilith and the Shekinah, indicating Lilith is the result of the *'uncovered'* Shekinah, created by the sins of the biblical Jews.   In an often overlooked but hugely significant passage it states:

> *"For the sin of unchastity Israel has been sent into captivity and the Shekinah also, and this is the uncovering of the Shekinah.  This unchastity is Lilith."*[125]

Even if this idea is considered to be original to the *Zohar*, rather than a continuation of older beliefs, this still places it at the thirteenth century, as the *Zohar* was published in 1290 CE.

From these later associations, it is clear that there is a link between Lilith and the Shekinah, however, this is more of a tangential and allegorical link, and should in no way be considered an equation of these two very different goddesses.

In contrast to this, the function of the goddess Inanna as the first recorded wisdom goddess in the Middle East heavily influences the likelihood that she was the precedent for subsequent wisdom goddesses, who commonly seem to draw on her characteristics.  The fact that a large Jewish community lived in Babylon for many centuries also reinforces the likelihood of cultural fertilisation from the earlier figure of Inanna and her subsequent manifestations as Ishtar and Astarte.  From here we now need to consider the goddesses of the people who became the Jews, the Semitic tribes.

---

125 Zohar I.27b, C13th CE.

# From the Semites

The term Semitic is used for a wide range of ancient tribes, including the Akkadians, Phoenicians, Ugarites and Hebrews. In this book we are specifically looking at the Semitic tribes who occupied Canaan in the period after the destruction of the Ugarites in the twelfth century BCE. These tribes were polytheistic, worshipping many different deities, in the centuries preceding the rise of Hebrew monotheism from around the seventh century BCE.

Amongst the Semitic deities there are two we need to particularly focus our attention on, the goddesses Anat and Astarte. Anat and Astarte were two goddesses who were part of the cross-fertilization process which took place between the religions and cultures of Egypt, Sumer and Canaan. By examining the motifs and deity connections associated with Anat and Astarte we shall consider whether either of these goddesses contributed to the development of the Wisdom Goddess and the Shekinah.

## Anat

Anat was a significant northwest Semitic deity who was reknowned for being a bloodthirsty virgin war goddess. This is illustrated by references to her in religious hymns from the region where she is described alongside piles of heads and palms. This describes the custom of collecting right hands to count the number of warriors killed, e.g. in KTU 1.3:

> *"Anat fought in the valley; she battled between the two towns. She smote the people of the sea-shore, she destroyed the men of the sunrise. Beneath her like balls were heads; above her like locusts were palms, like grasshoppers heaps of palms of warriors."*[126]

Although Semitic in origin and found in the Ugaritic texts from the fourteenth-twelfth century BCE, Anat also made the transition to Egypt along with the goddess Astarte. Both goddesses were frequently associated with each other, as illustrated in a Qudshu relief where they were equated with each other and Qudshu. Furthermore, in the Egyptian myths both Anat and Astarte were given to the Egyptian chaos god Seth as wives to placate him for losing the kingship to the Egyptian falcon-headed god Horus.

Anat was viewed by the Egyptians as one of the daughters of the sun god Ra. With her martial nature she was commonly depicted wielding a spear, battle axe and shield, and described as personally protecting the Pharaoh Ramesses III in battle.[127]

In the lost writings of the Phoenician priest Sakkunyaton (dated between eleventh-eighth centuries BCE), Anat was identified with the Greek wisdom goddess Athena, who was also a virgin war goddess (and was commonly depicted with shield and spear), emphasising the wisdom connection.

Although Anat is not mentioned by name in the Bible, there are references which hint at remnants of her worship.

---

126 Religious Texts From Ugarit, Wyatt, 2002:72-73.
127 The Complete Gods and Goddesses of Ancient Egypt, Wilkinson, 2003:137.

These traces of Anat are seen in place names like Beth-anath[128] (*'House of Anat'*) and Anathoth (plural of Anat).[129]

Anat was worshipped by the Elephantine Jews in Egypt as the Queen of Heaven (recalling Inanna and Astarte) under the name of Anatyahu (a merging of Anat with a derivative name drawn from Yahweh) in the fifth century BCE.[130] In another account of Anat from the same time period, she is described as Anat Bet-El (*'House of God'*).[131] In fact there were Neo-Assyrian references to the goddess Anat with this title from the seventh century BCE.[132]

The motif of light is associated with Anat in one of the Ugaritic texts, *A Hymn to Anat* (KTU 1.13), where she is described as being *"clothed in light"*.[133] This specific description of being clothed in light is one that would later be applied to Sophia in Gnostic texts.

A Cyprian inscription from the fourth century BCE equates Anat to the Greek wisdom goddess Athena (KAI 42), describing her as *"the strength of life"*, recalling the earlier equation of these two goddesses in the writings of the Phoenician priest Sakkunyaton. This combination of wisdom with martial skill is also seen in the earlier Ishtar, the Babylonian version of the Sumerian Inanna, first of the wisdom goddesses.

Another connection to the goddess Anat can be found in the Phoenician goddess Tanit, their form of Anat, who was worshipped especially at Carthage. In an interesting precursor to the subsequent Jewish depiction of the

---

128 Judges 1:33, C8th BCE; Joshua 15:59, Joshua 19:38, C7th-C6th BCE.
129 Joshua 21:18, 1 Kings 2:26, Isaiah 10:30, Jeremiah 1:1, all C7th-C6th BCE.
130 No Other Gods, Gnuse, 1997:185.
131 Is the Queen of Heaven in Jeremiah the Goddess Anat, Cohn, 2004.
132 Anat-Yahu, Some Other Deities, and the Jews of Elephantine, van der Toorn, 1992.
133 Religious Texts From Ugarit, Wyatt, 2002:172.

Shekinah, Tanit was described as *'Tanit Pene Baal'*, meaning *'the face of Baal'*.[134] Tanit was sometimes considered a lunar goddess, and this is seen in two inscriptions from the fifth and third century BCE at Athens equating Tanit with the Greek lunar virgin huntress goddess Artemis (KAI 53 and KAI 60).[135]

# Astarte

The Semitic goddess Astarte was worshipped by several tribes including the Phoenicians, Ugarites and Akkadians. The deity list in Ugaritic text RS 20.24 directly equates Ishtar and Astarte,[136] with Ishtar being the Semitic name for Inanna. Astarte (or Ashtart), like Qudshu was adopted by the Egyptians during the New Kingdom period (around 1200 BCE).

These goddesses, who were often conflated as manifestations of the same goddess, bear most of the same qualities. They were all linked to the planet Venus as the evening/morning star, they were all sexually powerful goddesses of fertility, love and war, and they were all depicted standing on the backs of lions, and were shown naked.

Astarte definitely maintained the bellicose qualities of her predecessor Ishtar, as seen in her presence in a peace treaty in 670 BCE, which proclaimed:

> *"May Ashtart break your bow in the thick of battle and have you crouch at the feet of your enemy."*[137]

---

134 The Virgin Goddess: Studies in the Pagan and Christian Roots of Mariology, Benko, 2003:23.
135 Literary Sources for the History of Palestine and Syria The Phoenician Inscriptions, Vance, 1994.
136 Ugaritica V, Schafer, 1939:45.
137 Neo-Assyrian Treaties and Loyalty Oaths, Parpola & Watanabe, 1988:27.

With the transmission of religious, social and cultural ideas in the ancient Middle East, it is easy to see how goddesses could be accepted and integrated into different countries, wearing a *'new set of clothes'*, as it were. Indeed, a reference to Inanna by the first recorded author in history, the priestess Enheduanna (circa 2300 BCE) says of the goddess that she *"wears the robes of the old, old gods"*,[138] indicating this development of deities with cultures.

Astarte is one of the goddesses who were mentioned in the *Old Testament*, though in a far more negative manner than Asherah. She is mentioned in association with King Solomon as the goddess he worshipped in his old age when he followed his loins, *"For Solomon followed Astarte the goddess of the Sidonians."*[139] This connection is repeated in the *Book of 2 Kings* which describes the desecration of sites associated with other gods and goddesses other than Yahweh.[140] There are also references to Astarte in the plural as Astartes, possibly suggesting statues, in *Judges* 2:13 and 10:6, *1 Samuel* 7:3-4 and 12:10.

Astarte would also take on another guise and be worshipped as Aphrodite by the Greeks, stepping out of the foam in her naked beauty, ruling over love and instigating wars. References from the writings of the Phoenician priest Sakkunyaton, who was said to have written somewhere between the eleventh and eight century BCE, equate Astarte and Aphrodite. His work only exists in fragments quoted by other later writers, though this view is also found in other sources, such as two second century BCE inscriptions from the Greek island of Delos to *"Palestinian Astarte, that is Aphrodite of the heavens."*[141]

---

138 Inanna, Lady of Largest Heart, Meador, 2000:15.
139 1 Kings 11:5, C7th BCE.
140 2 Kings 23:13, C7th BCE.
141 Inscriptions de Delos, ID 1719 & ID2305, Roussel & Launey, 1937.

A further syncretisation that occurred in Greek inscriptions is of Astarte with the Egyptian goddess Isis, as seen in a Cyprian dedication to *"Isis, Mother of the Deities, Ashtart"* (ID 2101).[142] A fourth century BCE Phoenician/Greek inscription found on a votive throne at Byblos equates Astarte with Isis-Hathor, with the words *"To the Lady of Byblos"* in Phoenician and *"Ashtart Great Goddess"* in Greek.[143] This syncretisation was also acknowledged by the first century CE Egyptian priest Isidorus in a temple inscription to Isis at Medinet Madi, saying *"The Syrians call you Ashtart-Artemis-Nanaia"*.[144]

Although not common, it is interesting to note that one inscription connects Astarte more closely with the god Baal, calling her *"Astarte-Name-of-Baal"* (KAI 14.18).[145] Baal of course was one of the gods who was considered to be a husband of Asherah, particularly by the Hebrews when they were trying to promote a negative image of Asherah.

References to Astarte continued into later literature, an example of which can be found in the work of John Milton. In his epic work *Paradise Lost* (1667) he writes illustrating how the names given to deities varied between cultures:

> *"Came Astoreth, whom the Phoenicians call'd*
> *Astarte, Queen of Heav'n, with crescent Horns;*
> *To whose bright Image nightly by the Moon*
> *Sidonian Virgins paid their Vows and Songs."*[146]

Having considered these goddesses, it is clear that Anat did have an influence on the development of the god

---

142 A Reconsideration of the Aphrodite-Ashtart Syncretisation, Budin, 2004:132.
143 Astarté: dossier documentaire et perspectives historiques, Bonnet, 1996:156
144 Supplementum Epigraphicum Graecum VIII, 1937:548, trans. Walbank, 1992.
145 The Inscriptions Written on Plaster at Kuntillet 'Ajrud, Mastin, 2009:111.
146 Paradise Lost, Book 1, Milton, 1667 CE.

Yahweh, being worshipped in places as his bride under the names Anatyahu and Anat Bet-El.

Furthermore, despite her original bloodthirsty nature, it is interesting to note that Anat was also equated with the Greek wisdom goddess Athena. In this context it seems possible that Anat did play a role in the development of the Shekinah, but in a peripheral sense as part of the process of maintaining the role of Yahweh's bride which was previously occupied by Asherah, and would subsequently be subsumed by the Wisdom Goddess and by the Shekinah.

The connection of Astarte to the development of the Shekinah is at best very tenuous. Whilst it is clear that Astarte was conflated with other goddesses, such as Inanna and Isis, the evidence does not seem to support a direct connection between her and the development of the Wisdom Goddess or the Shekinah.

Having considered the different goddesses who may have influenced the development of the Shekinah, the next step is to look at her contemporaries and possible descendants. In order to do this we will explore the Gnostic wisdom goddess Sophia in some detail, and also look at figures in Christianity and Islam who may have derived motifs and qualities from the Wisdom Goddess and the Shekinah.

# Part 3

# After the Fall

# Mother of Aeons

> *"Holy are you, Holy are you, Holy are you, Mother of the Aeons, Barbelo, for ever and ever, Amen."*
> ~ *Melchizidek, C4th CE, trans. Giversen & Pearson*

Gnosticism encompasses a diverse range of opinions, beliefs and practices, and does not represent one singular system of belief. The theology, cosmology and philosophy of ancient Gnosticism as perceived today are based on a number of extant texts, which clearly draw on not only early Judaic texts and Christianity, but also earlier Hellenistic sources. Within this there are further distinct schools of thought, with both shared and disparate views on divinity, man and the universe.

The early branches of Gnosticism (pre-fourth century CE) generally shared several views. These include the dualism of good and evil, with the material world viewed as being negative; a true higher god and inferior or false lower god; and a fall and redemption myth through a female divine power. This female divine power is most often called Sophia (*'wisdom'*, Greek) and is found in all the different strands of Gnosticism. Although the name Sophia is best known, different names were also sometimes used by different sects to refer to this female divinity; examples include Achamaoth, Barbelo and Edem.

Although there were numerous Gnostic groups, in the context of this book we specifically refer to the following three sects:

| Sect | First Mentioned in | Texts include |
|---|---|---|
| Ophite | Early 2nd century CE | *The Ophite Diagrams* |
| Sethian | 1st century CE (pre-Christian) | *Apocalypse of Zostrianos, Apocryphon of John, The Three Steles of Seth,* |
| Valentinian | Mid 2nd century CE | *Gospel of Truth, The Exegesis on the Soul, The Gospel of Philip* |

As most Gnostic works were written in the second-fourth century CE, which is around the same time that the first texts concerning the Shekinah were also written, we might expect a degree of cross-fertilisation of ideas between Sophia and the Shekinah. With the knowledge that they both derive from the Wisdom Goddess, we will look for areas of commonality between the Shekinah and the different forms of Sophia.

When examining the Gnostic texts, it is essential to take into account the gradual proliferation of *Old Testament* texts from the second century BCE to the first century CE and onwards. This point was made by Yamauchi (1978:154) when he observed, *"It is striking that for the most part the Gnostics' knowledge or at least use of the Old Testament is limited."*[147] This then suggests that many early Gnostics had little exposure or interest to the books of the *Old Testament*. However this was clearly not the case in later times, as witnessed by the numerous *Old Testament* references in the fourth century CE *Nag Hammadi* texts.

---

147 The Descent of Ishtar, the Fall of Sophia, and the Jewish Roots of Gnosticism, Yamauchi, 1978:154.

There are numerous parallels between the Cosmic Shekinah and Sophia, due to their common roots in the Wisdom Goddess, hence *"Sophia is joined in intimate union with God: she is his breath, emanation, reflection, image (Wisdom 7:25-26); the first of his creatures (Proverbs 8:22); his companion (Proverbs 8:30)."*[148] Additionally, the name Sophia is used in two different Gnostic strands to refer to the *'greater'* and *'lesser'* versions of the wisdom goddess, in the same way as the Cosmic or Heavenly (Greater) Shekinah and Earthly (Lesser) Shekinah.

Rather than Sophia, the Sethians and Ophites used the name Barbelo (which may be derived from the Coptic *berber* meaning *'boil over'*, *'seethe'* or *'overflow'*, hence *'great overflower'*) for the first emanation from the divine source. In their descriptions of Barbelo, she *"is the universal womb, She before everything"*,[149] recalling the description of the Wisdom Goddess in *Proverbs* and the Shekinah in *3 Enoch.*

Another suggested meaning of Barbelo is that it may have been derived from B-arba-Eloh, meaning *'In four is God'*, a reference to the Tetragrammaton (*'fourfold word'*, also known as the unpronounceable name of God). If this is the case it suggests an even stronger Jewish connection, as the Tetragrammaton is another name for Yahweh, the biblical husband of the Wisdom Goddess and then the Shekinah.[150]

Conversely it has also been argued that Barbelo is of unknown meaning, and is derived from *voces magicae* (magical names) found in the *Greek Magical Papyri,* such as Barbarelōcha (PGM XII.157) and Berbelōch (PGM Va.1). This argument is supported by the numerous other names found in Gnostic texts which are derived from *voces*

---

148 The Jewish Background of the Gnostic Sophia Myth, MacRae, 88.
149 Apocryphon of John, trans. Davies, C2nd CE.
150 Quoted from John Turner, in Voices of Gnosticism, Conner (ed.), 2011:86-87.

*magicae.*[151] The name of Sophia's son Ialdabaoth may also be derived from the *voces magicae* of the *Greek Magical Papyri*, with similar names such as Ialdazao (PGM IV.1195) and Aldabaeim occurring a number of times (PGM XIII.84, 153, 462, 596).

Barbelo is found in the higher or heavenly role in the *Nag Hammadi* texts, including the fourth century CE *Apocalypse of Zostrianos*. The *Apocalypse of Zostrianos* tells of the heavenly journey of the mystic Zostrianos, and includes his presentation to Barbelo by the female angel Yoel. The *Apocalypse of Zostrianos*, like some of the other Gnostic texts, shows clear derivation from earlier Merkavah texts which are full of Shekinah motifs, particularly the *Book of 3 Enoch*. The angel Yoel is an example of this, being one of the seventy names for the archangel Metatron, who is particularly associated with the Shekinah in Merkavah literature.

Another name for Barbelo which is found in some Gnostic texts is Ennoia (*'thought'*, Greek). The emphasis on light and glory in association with Ennoia bring to mind the inherent connection between the Shekinah and light, and her alternative title of Kavod, meaning *'glory'*:

> *"His self-aware thought (ennoia) came into being.*
> *Appearing to him in the effulgence of his light.*
> *She stood before him*
> *This, then, is the first of the powers, prior to everything.*
> *Arising out of the mind of the Father*
> *The Providence (pronoia) of everything.*
> *Her light reflects His light.*
> *She is from His image in His light*
> *Perfect in power*
> *Image of the invisible perfect Virgin Spirit.*
> *She is the initial power*

---

151 The Origin in Ancient Incantatory "Voces Magicae" of Some Names in the Sethian Gnostic System, Jackson, 1989

*glory of Barbelo*
*glorious among the realms*
*glory of revelation*
*She gave glory to the Virgin Spirit*
*She praised Him, For she arose from Him.*
*[This, the first Thought, is the Spirit's image]*
*She is the universal womb*
*She is before everything"*[152]

The church father Iraneus (C2nd CE) in his anti-Gnostic text *Against Heresies* describes how, as Ennoia, Sophia also takes the role of mother to Jesus.[153] However, as with other anti-Gnostic texts, we have to treat the information carefully due to its hostile bias.

The author G.R.S. Mead (1863-1933 CE) lists many of the names attributed to Sophia in the Gnostic texts, expressing many of her qualities. It is interesting to compare these and see which titles are shared with the Shekinah or describe her qualities, such as Daughter of Light, Eden, Paradise, All-Mother, Mother of the Living, Hidden Mother, the Power Above, and Holy Spirit:

> *"It is not surprising, then, that we should find the Sophia in her various aspects possessed of many names. Among these may be mentioned the Mother, or All-Mother; Mother of the Living, or Shirting Mother; the Power Above; the Holy Spirit; again, She of the Left-hand as opposed to the Christos, Him of the Right-hand; the Man-woman; Prouneikos or Lustful one; the Matrix; Paradise; Eden; Achamōth; the Virgin; Barbēlō; Daughter of Light; Merciful Mother; Consort of the Masculine One; Revelant of the Perfect Mysteries; Perfect Mercy; Revelant of the Mysteries of the whole Magnitude; Hidden Mother; She who knows the Mysteries of the*

---

152 Apocryphon of John, trans. Davies, C2nd CE.
153 Against Heresies, Book 2, Iraneus, 180 CE.

> *Elect; the Holy Dove who has given birth to Twins; Ennœa; Ruler; and the Lost or Wandering Sheep, Helena, and many other names.*"[154]

In one version of the Gnostic theology, it is Sophia who causes the earth to be, the *'fall'*, and the redemption of the earth. Sophia was viewed as the lower emanation, who caused the earth to be formed from her desire rather than following the divine plan. This equates to the Sephira of Malkuth in Kabbalah, which is the Earthly Shekinah.

Furthermore, Sophia's light was then hidden in Adam and his offspring, paralleling the idea of the Shekinah being present within all of us as the higher soul (Neshamah), the scattered sparks of her divine light:

> *"And immediately Sophia stretched forth her finger and introduced Light into Matter, and she pursued it down to the region of Chaos."*[155]

This idea of the light of the soul is seen in other Gnostic texts, for example in the *Apocryphon of John* we see that *"Barbelo conceived and bore a spark of light"*.[156] The light reference also recurs in the Manichean religion, which flourished in the Middle and Far East from the third-seventh century CE and beyond in some areas. Manichaeism is often likened to a branch of Gnosticism, and according to Saint Ephrem described the soul in terms of light as, *"the refined soul which they say is the daughter of light."*[157] Manichean texts also referred to Sophia as *"the Virgin of Light, the chief of all excellencies."*[158]

---

154 Fragments of a Faith Forgotten, Mead, 1900:334-335.
155 The Hypostasis of the Archons, C4th CE, trans. Robinson, 1977:158.
156 Apocryphon of John, trans. Davies, C2nd CE.
157 St Ephrem I.71, C4th CE.
158 Turfan fragment M172, C8th-C10th CE.

The Gnostic strand of Valentinism used the name Sophia for the higher or *'greater'* heavenly manifestation, and Achamaoth (possibly derived from the Hebrew *Chokmah*, meaning *'wisdom'*) for the *'lesser'* or earthly manifestation. Some Valentinian texts describe Achamaoth resisting the unfolding of the divine pattern of the aeons due to her overwhelming love of God and desire to remain close to him, resulting in the manifestation of the physical world.

In the Valentinian strand Jesus redeems the earth rather than Sophia, and he and Achamaoth will eventually be bride and groom, mirroring the higher pairing of Sophia and God. The father and mother, daughter and son couples here clearly parallel the attributions of the letters of Tetragrammaton, and its Kabbalistic associations with the Shekinah as both mother and daughter.

In *The First Apocalypse of James*, Achamaoth is referred to as the daughter of Sophia, the lower emanation, but also as having no father. Through parthenogenesis Sophia created Achamaoth, the implication being that the lack of male balance caused her actions:

> *"But I shall call upon the imperishable knowledge, which is Sophia who is in the Father (and) who is the mother of Achamaoth. Achamaoth had no father nor male consort, but she is female from a female."*[159]

A number of Gnostic texts describe Ialdabaoth, the son of Sophia, whom she produced in her desire to create from herself, for she *"wanted to bring forth a likeness out of herself without the consent of the Spirit"*.[160] Other Gnostic texts describe the process with more emphasis on Sophia's pre-eminence:

---

159 The First Apocalypse of James, Nag Hammadi Library, trans. Schoedel, C4th CE.
160 The Apocryphon of John, Nag Hammadi Library, trans. Robinson, 1977:103-4.

> *"Sophia, the Mother of the Universe and the consort, desired by herself to bring these to existence without her male (consort)."*[161]

Ialdabaoth is described as the first of the seven archons ('rulers'), who are the lowest emanation of the divine and are often considered demonic. Significantly Ialdabaoth is often described as leonine and lion-headed, recalling the earlier association between lions and the Sumerian goddess Inanna, the Canaanite goddess Asherah, and the Chaldean Hekate (who is named as one of the archons in *Pistis Sophia*).

All of these attributions and numerous other qualities of the Sophia and the Shekinah are found in the third-fourth century CE text of *The Thunder, Perfect Mind*, found amongst the *Nag Hammadi* texts. This text, which may date back as far as the first century BCE,[162] takes the form of strophes (parallel stanzas) where contradictory qualities are claimed. Although the female divinity is not named, it is clearly Sophia being referred to, as the list of qualities in this extract shows:

> *"I am the mother and the daughter.*
> *I am the bride and the bridegroom,*
> *and it is my husband who begot me.*
> *I am the silence that is incomprehensible*
> *and the idea whose remembrance is frequent.*
> *I am the voice whose sound is manifold*

---

161 The Sophia of Jesus Christ, Nag Hammadi Library, trans. Robinson, 1977:225.
162 Jewish Gnosis and Mandean Gnosticism, Quispel, 1975:105.

*and the word whose appearance is multiple.*
*I am the utterance of my name."*[163]

One of the most striking features of *The Thunder, Perfect Mind* is the references to Sophia as *"the whore and the holy one"*.[164] This is a theme repeated in other Gnostic texts, such as *The Second Treatise of the Great Seth*, which states *"our sister Sophia - she who is a whore"*.[165] Sophia was also referred to with the epithet Prounikos (*'lustful'*, Greek), becoming Sophia Prounikos, literally *'Wisdom the lustful'* or *'Wisdom the whore'*. Rather than assuming this is a sexual interpretation, or an insult, a possible interpretation of Sophia's lust could be the lust to create, which produces the material world, or Kabbalistic Malkuth.

It has been suggested by some scholars that the descent of Sophia into matter, and by implication that of the Shekinah, are derived from the earlier Sumerian myth of the Descent of Inanna.[166] If this is the case they have both changed considerably, though the planetary nature of the seven archons of Sophia, and the descent of the Shekinah through the seven planetary heavens to earth and her return to heaven can be seen as possible derivatives of Inanna's descent through the seven gates of the underworld and back up again.

Another possible antecedent for the fall of Sophia is the fall of Eve in the *Old Testament*.[167] When Eve eats the fruit of the Tree of Life (*Genesis 3:6*) she initiates the *'Fall'* by gaining wisdom. One of the *Nag Hammadi* texts equates

---

163 The Thunder, Perfect Mind, Nag Hammadi Library, trans. MacRae, C3rd-C4th CE.
164 The Thunder, Perfect Mind, Nag Hammadi Library, trans. MacRae C3rd-C4th CE.
165 The Second Treatise of the Great Seth, Nag Hammadi Library, trans. Bullard & Gibbons, C4th CE.
166 E.g. Bousset (1907), Knox (1937), Glasson (1954), Grant (1966).
167 MacRae also suggests this in The Jewish Background of the Gnostic Sophia Myth.

Eve with Zoe ('life', Greek), the daughter of Sophia, and retells Genesis with a radical twist.[168] In this Gnostic version, the creation of the demiurge Ialdabaoth from Pistis Sophia is described, along with all the subsequent beings Ialdabaoth generates. Eve exists before Adam in this tale, and initiates him into wisdom through the consumption of the fruit of the Tree of Life, which she had entered, leaving her likeness with him. Eve as a more powerful being than Adam is also indicated in other texts, e.g. Adam saying to Seth, *"with Eve, your mother, I went about with her in a glory which she had seen in the aeon from which we had come forth. She taught me a word of knowledge of the eternal God."*[169]

Another form of Sophia found in Gnostic texts is that of Edem in the second century BCE *Book of Baruch*. Edem is probably derived from the Hebrew *Adamah*, meaning 'Earth', and may also be drawn from Eden. With its early date the *Book of Baruch* significantly predates most other Gnostic texts by centuries. As such the flavour is more reminiscent of the Biblical Wisdom Goddess and the Shekinah, rather than of Sophia, e.g. the equation of the divine feminine to Israel.

In the *Book of Baruch*, Edem and Elohim first create he earth and twenty-four angels (twelve each), and then humanity. The third angel created by Elohim was called Baruch ('the Blessed One') and associated with the Tree of Life, and the third angel created by Edem was called Naas ('Snake') and associated with the Tree of Knowledge of Good and Evil.

However Elohim ascends to the Higher God, who shows him the imperfection of his creation and keeps him in heaven. The rejected Edem then introduces various ills onto humanity in punishment (part two of the *Book of*

---

168 On the Origin of the World, Nag Hammadi Library, trans. Bethge & Layton.
169 The Apocalypse of Adam, Nag Hammadi Library, trans. MacRae, C4th CE.

*Baruch*). Significantly Edem *"is earth; garden; Israel; creator of humans, beasts and the soul; and a symbol of Eve, who is her creation and double"*.[170] The titles of Edem are reminiscent of the Shekinah as well as of Sophia, as is the serpentine connection mentioned in the description of Edem as *"half virgin and half viper"*.[171]

As Marcovitch (1988:95) points out, the half human with a serpentine body is the shape of the Echidna in Greek mythology, recalling the Hellenistic influence which occurred in Gnosticism.[172] This connection was claimed by Hippolytus in the second century CE in his *Refutation of All Heresies*.

However another possible, and perhaps more likely, influence on the figure of Edem is that of the goddess Isis-Hermouthis, who was also depicted as a woman with a serpent's body. Several temples were erected specifically to her during the Hellenistic period (323-146 BCE), and in four Greek hymns to Isis from this time *"Hermouthis is equated with Isis and praised as goddess of fertility, as Panthea, as Bona Fortuna, as bearer of Maat, and as the unique one."*[173] This combination of qualities, particularly bearer of Ma'at and unique one, give strong support to Isis-Hermouthis as the origin of Edem's form.

Hippolytus quoted the Gnostic Justinus in his *Refutation of All Heresies*, saying:

> *"When therefore, you hear men asserting that the swan went in unto Leda and begat a child from her, know that the swan is Elohim and Leda, Edem. And when people allege that an*

170 The Gnostic Bible, Barnstone & Meyer, 2003:108.
171 Justin's Baruch: A Showcase of Gnostic Syncretism, Marcovitch, 1988:95.
172 Justin's Baruch: A Showcase of Gnostic Syncretism, Marcovitch, 1988:95.
173 The Shape of Edem according to Justin the Gnostic, Van Den Broek, 1973:39.

> *eagle went in unto Ganymede, know that the
> eagle is Naas, and Ganymede, Adam."*[174]

This interesting piece of symbolic explanation may, as King (1933:71) suggests, explain *"the Coptic preoccupation with the theme of Leda and the Swan"*.[175] Of more interest though are the equation of Gnostic themes to classical Greek myth; and also the equation of the eagle and the snake, a theme which would be found in association with the elements in ceremonial magic in the last two centuries.

The *Wedding Hymn* of the *Acts of Thomas* (second century CE) demonstrates how some of Sophia's motifs may have been derived from the Wisdom Goddess and/or Shekinah and may have been influenced by other goddesses. Marcovich (1981:156-73) argues convincingly for the *Wedding Hymn* being a Valentinian Gnostic text, but points out there are some puzzling discrepancies.[176]

An interesting reference in line 5, which reads *"Truth rests upon her head"*, strongly hints at the influence of the Egyptian Goddess Maat, with her feather of truth upon her head.

Additionally the phrase *"The Bride is the Daughter of Light"* (line 1) hints at a possible Manichean influence, as this is one of the common titles of the divine feminine in Manichaeism.

There are numerous elements in the text which point to the influence of the *Wisdom of Solomon*, and intriguingly some which hint at a Kabbalistic influence. Thus we see reference to *"Thirty-two are they who sing praises in her"* (line 7), which suggests the thirty-two paths of the Tree of Life, and also the line from *Sepher Yetzirah*, *"With thirty-two*

---

174 Refutation of All Heresies, Hippolytus, C2nd CE.
175 Some Reliefs at Budapest, King, 1933:71.
176 The Wedding Hymn of Actae Thomae, 1981, Marcovich, 156-173.

*mystical paths of wisdom engraved Yah".*[177] This Kabbalistic attribution is substantiated a few lines later with the line *"Her ten fingers open the gates of the city"* (line 11), a clear allusion to the ten Sephiroth of the Tree of Life, which were often likened to fingers, with the gate of the city being the pathway to God.

The line *"On the crown of her head sits the King, feeding with his ambrosia those who sit beneath him"* (line 4) also suggests the Kabbalah, as the highest Sephira of the Tree of Life is Kether – the crown. The idea that the king is feeding those beneath with his ambrosia is similar to the idea of the other Sephiroth being fed with the divine emanations from Kether.[178]

This interesting set of symbols and motifs is particularly significant when we consider the absence of Kabbalistic texts, with the exception of the *Sepher Yetzirah* until the Medieval period, and argues for the influence of either oral Kabbalistic teachings or (more likely) the *Sepher Yetzirah* on some areas of Gnosticism.

The unnamed divine feminine in the fourth century CE *Trimorphic Protennoia* is clearly Sophia, and the wide-ranging descriptions in this text are similar in some respects to the scope of the text *Thunder, Perfect Mind*, in that they could equally be describing the Shekinah:

> *"I am Protennoia, the Thought that dwells in the Light. I am the movement that dwells in the All, she in whom the All takes its stand, the first-born among those who came to be, she who exists before the All. She (Protennoia) is called by three names, although she dwells alone, since she is perfect. I am invisible within the Thought of the Invisible One. I am revealed in the immeasurable, ineffable (things). I am*

---

177 Sepher Yetzirah 1.1, C2nd CE.
178 Climbing the Tree of Life, Rankine, 2005:48, 85.

> *incomprehensible,     dwelling     in     the*
> *incomprehensible. I move in every creature."*[179]

A more recent perception of Sophia which also draws on the Shekinah was expressed by the nineteenth century Russian theologian Vladimir Solov'ev. In his writings he identified Sophia as the partner of God the logos, calling her *"The body of God, she is also the soul of the world, the incarnated divine idea."*[180] That Solov'ev was drawing on the early portrayals of the Shekinah in his more Gnostic use of the term Sophia, is seen in his reference to sources such as the Biblical book of *Proverbs* and the *Wisdom of Solomon.*[181] It is also seen when he writes on the Shekinah, calling her *"the divine power and glory".*[182]

Rather than one coming from the other, it seems more likely that the Shekinah and Sophia are different embodiments of the Wisdom Goddess arising from the same sources acted upon by different influences. In the case of the Shekinah these influences include the Canaanite, Egyptian, and Sumerian/Babylonian cultures, with Sophia being more heavily influenced by Hellenic, Jewish and Christian cultures.

In this Sophia may be seen as being the more derivative from the other, as the Jewish culture which produced the Shekinah also influenced the development of Sophia. Both the Shekinah and Sophia influenced the development of Christian literature, as we shall see in the following chapter *The Christian and Islamic Goddess.*

---

179 Trimorphic Protennoia, C4th CE, trans. J.D. Turner.
180 Chteniia 3:127, 146, Solov'ev.
181 Solov'ev's Androgynous Sophia and the Jewish Kabbalah, Kornblatt, 1991.
182 Chteniia 11:322, Solov'ev.

# The Christian & Islamic Goddess

In addition to being influenced by her antecedents and contemporaries, the Shekinah also produced and influenced later derivative manifestations of the divine feminine wisdom. These include the Holy Spirit and Virgin Mary of Christianity; and Sakina in Islam, each of which show clear associations to the Shekinah and who assimilated at least some of her characteristics.

## Holy Spirit

The translation of Shekinah into the Holy Spirit is beautifully illustrated in a hymn written by the fourth century CE theologian Ephrem the Syrian (Saint Ephrem, 306-373 CE). In his hymn 11, he wrote:

> *"Give thanks,*
> *O Daughter whose crowns are two!*
> *Thy temples and thy children rejoice.*
> *For see,*
> *the hallowing of thy temples in worship,*
> *And the hallowing of thy children by anointing!*
> *Blessed art thou,*
> *for at once there began in thee*

> *The Shekinah for thy inhabitants;*
> *The Spirit descended on thy children."*

It was not only Christian writers who made this connection between the Holy Spirit and the Shekinah, with the Jewish Kabbalist Judah ben Barzillai in the twelfth century CE observing, *"He created as the first of all of His creations the holy spirit, which is also called the Glory of our God ... and the sages call this great light Shekinah."*[183]

The German Abbess Hildegard von Bingen (1098-1179 CE), also known as the Sibyl of the Rhine, writing on *The Holy Spirit as Caritas* (grace) described it in a way which is clearly reminicent of both the Wisdom Goddess and the Shekinah. This is perhaps not so surprising when the prevalent influence of wisdom texts like the *Wisdom of Solomon, Proverbs* and *Jesus Sirach* in medieval theology is taken into consideration:

> *"I flame above the beauty of the fields to signify the earth -- the matter from which humanity was made. I shine in the waters to indicate the soul, for, as water suffuses the whole earth, the soul pervades the whole body. I burn in the sun and the moon to denote Wisdom, and the stars are the innumerable words of Wisdom."*[184]

Hildegard von Bingen was very emphatic in the way she described the Holy Spirit, and there are clear similarities between the way in which she viewed the Holy Spirit and descriptions of the Shekinah, Sophia and other wisdom goddesses. In her work *The Holy Spirit as Wisdom: Scientia Dei (Knowledge of God)* she emphasises concepts such as divine wisdom, omnipotence in both heaven and

---

183 Commentary on Sepher Yetzirah, Judah Ben Barzillai, C12th CE.
184 Sister of Wisdom: St Hildegard's Theology of the Feminine, Newman, 1997:70.

earth, radiance, brightness and splendour, which are all familiar concepts associated with the Shekinah.

> *"She is Divine Wisdom. She watches over all people and all things in heaven and on earth, being of such radiance and brightness that, for the measureless splendour that shines in Her, you cannot gaze on Her face or on the garments She wears. For She is awesome in terror as the Thunderer's lightening, and gentle in goodness as the sunshine. Hence, in Her terror and Her gentleness, She is incomprehensible to mortals, because of the dread radiance of divinity in Her face and the brightness that dwells in Her as the robe of Her beauty. She is like the Sun, which none can contemplate in its blazing face or in the glorious garment of its rays. For She is with all and in all, and of beauty so great in Her mystery that no one could know how sweetly She bears with people, and with what unfathomable mercy She spares them."*[185]

# Virgin Mary

The role of the Virgin Mary is one which has caused a huge amount of division within Christianity over the centuries. Early Eastern Christianity was quick to venerate the Virgin Mary, and this was already established by the fifth century CE at the council of Ephesus (431 CE).

One of the Church fathers, Saint Cyril of Alexandria set the template for the association between the god-bearing Mary and the divine wisdom which would be called Shekinah or Sophia. Though his description of Mary could grace many of the goddesses of the ancient world, it is

---

185 Sister of Wisdom: St Hildegard's Theology of the Feminine, Newman, 1997:47.

particularly reminiscent of the Shekinah and the Gnostic Sophia as the redemptrix:

> *"Through her heaven rejoices; through her angels and archangels are pleased; through her demons are chased away; through her the devil, the tempter, fell from heaven; through her the whole of creation will be taken up into heaven; through her the whole of creation, which was caught up in idolatry, came to recognise the truth."*[186]

The relationship between the divine feminine wisdom and the Virgin Mary is further emphasised in the Gnostic text *Pistis Sophia* (probably written during the late third century CE). This text describes Jesus as saying to his mother Mary:

> *"They shall proclaim thee blessed from one end of the earth to the other; for the pledge of the First Mystery hath taken up its abode with thee, and through that pledge shall all from the earth and all from the height be saved, and that pledge is the beginning and the end."*[187]

A sixth century text pseudoepigraphically attributed to bishop Melito of Saris went even further in making the direct link between Mary and the Shekinah through the titles given to her by Jesus when he resurrects Mary, calling her *"my dove, tent of glory, vessel of life, heavenly temple."*[188] The dove reference is particularly interesting when considering the dove as a symbol of the Holy Spirit at the baptism of Jesus. The tent of glory and heavenly temple are both clear Shekinah references.

---

186 Homiliae Diversae 4:991-2, Cyril, trans. Schwartz.
187 Pistis Sophia, Mead, 1921:98.
188 Pseudo-Melito, C6th CE, trans. Haibach-Reinisch.

The Gnostics called on Mary at times, and one example of a phylactery (amulet tied to the arm) to protect from demons in *Oriental MS 5987* goes so far as to have the speaker identifying with Mary. This would therefore seem to be a more cosmic Mary drawing on the Sophia/Shekinah:

> *"For I am Mary, who is hidden in the appearance of Miriam. I am the mother who has given birth to the true light."*[189]

The veneration of the Virgin Mary is clearly seen in the sixth century *Akathist Hymn to the Theotokos*, which is still used today. The titles and descriptions given to Mary are so clearly duplicating earlier attributions to the Shekinah and her antecedents that they are worth mentioning to demonstrate their scope.

They include:

- the King's throne
- Star revealing the Sun, through whom creation is renewed,
- heavenly Ladder, by which God descended,
- Bridge leading those from earth to Heaven,
- knowledge superseding the wise,
- you through whom we are clothed with glory,
- Tree of delectable Fruit that nourishes the faithful,
- well-shaded Tree under which many find shelter,
- she kindles the celestial Light and leads all to divine knowledge,
- she illuminates our minds with radiance,
- Ark made golden by the Spirit.

---

189 Ancient Christian Magic, Meyer & Smith, 1999:131.

This veneration of Mary as the principle of wisdom and/or bride of God became more pronounced in the Western Church from the eleventh to twelfth century CE through the work of individuals such as Peter Damian, Herman of Tournay (who went as far as calling Mary the bridegroom of God), Bernard of Clairvaux (who equated Mary to the woman clothed with the Sun), Godfrey of Admont, Hildegard von Bingen and Peter of Blois (who called Mary the Queen of Heaven and Rose of Sharon).

The view was propagated by some writers like Hildegard von Bingen that effectively Mary was the new Eve, repairing the damage caused by the original sin. In this Mary's existence became merged with the Shekinah, and she was given a predicted role before creation, as *"the shining white lily on which God gazed before all creation."*[190]

# Sakina

In Islam the Shekinah is known as Sakina, and the importance of the Sakina (derived from the word Shekinah and meaning *'peace'* or *'tranquillity'*, with a secondary meaning which mirrors the Hebrew of *'to abide or inhabit'*) should not be underestimated.

In the stories of the founding of Mecca, the patriarch Abraham was guided on his journey by the Shekinah, who directed him where to build. Significantly the Shekinah was said to have marked the spot for Abraham by curling up like a serpent.[191] The serpent imagery here is reminiscent of the Egyptian Goddess Qudshu, the Gnostic Edem as well as the serpent of wisdom or temptation in the Garden of Eden.

---

190 Symphonia, Hildegard of Bingen, 1170 CE.
191 Journeys in Holy Lands: the Evolution of the Abraham-Ishamel Legends in Islamic Exegesis, Firestone, 1990:68-71.

The term Sakina and its derivatives are used a number of times in the *Qur'an* (16:80, 48:4, 48:18, 48:26), and significantly even in connection with tree symbolism:

> *"Allah's Good Pleasure was on the Believers when they swore Fealty to thee under the Tree: He knew what was in their hearts, and He sent down Sakina [tranquillity] to them; and He rewarded them with a speedy Victory;"*[192]

The presence of the Sakina as a source of inspiration is emphasised in the *Qur'an*, with a slightly different derivative focus:

> *"He it is Who sent down the Sakina into the hearts of the believers that they might add faith unto their faith"*[193]

The tangible presence of the Shekinah is also something found in common between Christianity and Islam, as illustrated by Sufi biographies, where the enveloping radiance of the Sakina is equated to the halo of Christian saints. Thus we see in the tales of Rabi'a, the female Muslim mystic, that *"While she was still praying, he saw a lamp above her head, suspended without a chain, and the whole house was illuminated by the rays from that light."*[194]

Flashes of light were also seen as being indicative of angelic visitation in the sanctuary of a temple in the process of achieving Sakina. Thus *"when the presence of these lights is prolonged – when they become permanently present – the state attained is designated by Suhravardī as Sakīnah. This word is precisely the equivalent of the Hebrew*

---

192 Qur'an 48:18, C7th CE.
193 Qur'an 48:4, C7th CE.
194 Rabi'a the mystic & her fellow saints in Islam, Smith, 1984:7.

*Shekinah: the mysterious divine presence in the Holy of Holies in the Temple of Solomon.*"[195]

It is clear that there was direct influence from the Shekinah into Christianity and Islam, with motifs and titles being assimilated into figures such as the Holy Spirit, the Virgin Mary and the Sakina. Even if this link is not often acknowledged, it is one which we have clearly demonstrated and cannot be ignored.

---

195 Temple and Contemplation, Corbin, 1986:274.

# Parallel Wisdom

As well as the goddesses who directly influenced the development of the Shekinah, or who were directly influenced by her, there are also several other goddesses who seem to exhibit similar characteristics and roles. In this section we will consider some of these goddesses, in particular those who share the role of wisdom goddess and goddess of souls with the Shekinah. We are not suggesting that there are any direct connection between the goddesses in this section and the Shekinah, but rather that it is interesting to note the similarities between these goddesses and the Shekinah.

# Hekate

Hekate was worshipped from at least around the eighth century BCE when her name is first found in ancient Greek literature in the *Theogony* of Hesiod. Although her origins are uncertain, her worship would continue through the Roman and Byzantine empires for many centuries through into the Dark Ages. This ancient goddess was viewed, like the Shekinah, as both the world soul and the source of souls.

In the *Chaldean Oracles* (second century CE), Hekate is clearly described in terms which mirror those of the

Shekinah and Yahweh, as bestower of divine wisdom from the Greek god Zeus as the all-father.

Furthermore, like the Shekinah she has a strong connection with angels, indeed she is the *"source of angels, demons, souls and natures."*[196] The *Chaldean Oracles* describes Hekate as ruling over three orders of angels called the Iynges (*'Wrynecks'*, after the bird), Synocheis (*'Connectors'*) and Teletarchai (*'Rulers'*). The *Greek Magical Papyri* also mention the connection between Hekate and angels, in the *Lunar Spell of Claudianus* where Hekate-Selene is asked to *"send forth your angel from among those who assist you"*.[197]

There is reference to heavenly and earthly forms of Hekate, again paralleling the Shekinah. The lower earthly aspect of Hekate, called Physis (*'Nature'*, Greek) is described in the *Chaldean Oracles* thus, *"From the back of the Goddess is suspended boundless Nature"*.[198] However, to the Theurgists, like the Gnostics, the earthly was not to be sought, hence the *Oracles* warned *"Invoke not the actually visible image of Nature"* and *"Gaze not upon Nature, for Her name is Fate"*.[199]

Hekate may also be seen as a wisdom goddess, this being emphasised in the *Chaldean Oracles* where it records that *"Amongst the Immortal Gods Hekate has never said to the wise spokesmen of the Gods anything vain or unfulfilled ... She is always irradiated by Truth."*[200]

The Gnostics however did not view Hekate as a wisdom goddess, but instead named her as one of the five rulers or archons, which may be seen as part of the process of demonising the older deities. It is interesting to note that the Gnostics referred specifically to Hekate Triformis, as

---

196 The Goddess Hekate, Ronan, 1992:94.
197 PGM VII.862-918, C3rd-C4th CE.
198 The Goddess Hekate, Ronan, 1992:94.
199 Ibid, 1992:99.
200 Ibid, 1992: 98.

many of the references to her in this form, such as the *Greek Magical Papyri*, describe her with animal heads.

> "The third order is called Triple-faced Hekatē, and there are under her authority seven-and-twenty [arch]demons, and it is they which enter into men and seduce them to perjuries and lies and to covet that which doth not belong to them."[201]

A parallel does exist from Hekate to the Gnostics, in the fourth century CE Gnostic text *Trimorphic Protennoia*, with some of the phrases found within that text recalling the qualities of Chaldean Hekate:

> "I am the movement that dwells in the All, she in whom the All takes its stand, the first-born among those who came to be, she who exists before the All. She is called by three names, although she dwells alone, since she is perfect."[202]

Another similarity between the Chaldean Hekate and the Shekinah can be found in references to her fiery splendour, described in her visible manifestations. Thus her appearance *"when you see the formless and very holy fire radiantly leaping up throughout the depths of the whole world: hear the Voice of Fire"*.[203]

One of the theories regarding the origin of the Goddess Hekate, is that she may derive from the Minoan Serpent Goddess.[204] This is an interesting parallel when we consider the possible associations already discussed between the Minoan Snake Goddess and the goddesses Asherah and Qudshu.

---

201 Pistis Sophia, Mead, 1921:304.
202 Trimorphic Protennoia, C4th CE, trans. Turner.
203 Ibid, 1992:102.
204 Hekate Her Sacred Fires, d'Este, 2010:32.

# Metis

Metis (*'Wise Counsel'*) was a Titan wisdom goddess, the daughter of the goddess Tethys and the god Oceanus. She was the first wife of the Olympian sky god Zeus, who advised him and had the ability to shapeshift into any form. After hearing a prophecy that his children by Metis would supersede him, Zeus tricked Metis into assuming the form of a fly and swallowed her to prevent her from having children.

Faraone and Teeter (2004) have suggested quite convincingly that Metis was derived from the Egyptian goddess Ma'at.[205]  Both goddesses represent abstracts (wisdom, truth, kingship) required by the ruling male gods. The association with kingship is well documented in the case of Ma'at, and in addition to the references in Hesiod's *Theogony*, a reference in the fifth century BCE *Derweni Papyrus* attributes *'kingly office'* to Metis.

After the consumption of Metis, Zeus subsequently gave birth to Athena, the goddess of wisdom who sprang forth fully formed from his head. In response to this his jealous wife Hera mimicked him and brought forth Typhon, a monstrous storm-giant. Typhon was cast into the hell of Tartarus by Zeus. This pattern is repeated in the Ophian and Sethite strands of Gnosticism, told in the *Hypostasis of the Archons*, with Sophia being jealous of God's ability to create from himself, and producing the monstrous demiurge Ialdabaoth, who was also cast down.[206]

---

205 Egyptian Maat and Hesiodic Metis, Faraone & Teeter, 2004.
206 A Classical Influence on the Gnostic Sophia Myth, Goehring, 20.

# Shakti

In parallel with the Shekinah and her earlier manifestations, there was another goddess being worshipped in another part of the world who manifested through many forms, the Indian Shakti (or Śakti). Shakti means *'power'* or *'energy'*, and she is viewed as the cosmic power or energy which creates change.

Significantly, Shakti is *"treated both as a goddess and a philosophical category"*,[207] paralleling the way the Shekinah is often perceived. However unlike the Shekinah, Shakti is perceived as being the essence of every goddess.

Like the Shekinah, she has a cosmic or Heavenly manifestation, and also an Earthly manifestation within everyone, as the kundalini, or serpent fire power. This is described as a sleeping serpent coiled three and a half times at the base of the spine. Through spiritual discipline and activity, the kundalini (divine feminine within) can be awoken, and journey up the spine, piercing the six energy centres (called chakras, meaning *'wheels'*) which are situated there until she reaches the crown, where the seventh major chakra is positioned. Here she unites with the sleeping Shiva (divine masculine within), creating bliss through their union, which is said to manifest as a divine flow of water back down to the base of the spine.

---

207 Śakti: The Power in Tantra, Tigunait, 1998:7.

# Part 4

# Behold,
# She is the Tree of Life

# The Tree of Life

*"Hope deferred makes the heart sick, but a desire fulfilled is a tree of life."*
~ *Proverbs 13:12, C3rd BCE*

The Kabbalah is a Jewish system of magical philosophy and spiritual practice which syncretised components of Gnosticism, Neo-Platonism, and early Jewish mysticism (Merkavah mysticism) with aspects of ancient Sumerian and Egyptian cosmologies. These diverse sources all came together in tenth-fourteenth century Europe, although their origins were considerably older.

Due to its early oral origins, the first appearance of the Kabbalah cannot be specifically dated. Considering the word Kabbalah means *'received wisdom'*, this oral beginning is entirely appropriate. The *Sepher Yetzirah* (*Book of Formation*), one of the key texts on which Kabbalistic philosophy is based, is usually regarded as being dated to the second-third century CE.[208]

However, the first known written reference to the ten Sephiroth, which are key to the Kabbalah, has been dated to around 70 CE in the early *Haggigah* material which

---

208 This dating is thoroughly argued in Some Observations on Sefer Yesira (1) Its Use of Scripture, Hayman, 1984.

contributed to the *Talmud* (Rabbinical religious, legal and ethical lore), where some of the Sephirothic names were recorded:

> "*Ten agencies through which God created the world, vis, wisdom, insight, cognition, strength, power, inexorableness, justice, right, lore, mercy.*"[209]

It is interesting to see that the first of the names mentioned is wisdom, hinting at the pre-eminence of wisdom (and hence the Shekinah) even at this time. Although the Kabbalah as a named system would not emerge for many centuries after the *Haggigah*, its development can be seen as expressing the manifestation of the wisdom of the Shekinah.

The philosophies and practices of the original Jewish Kabbalah, including the Shekinah, have blown like seeds and blossomed in a wide range of magical and spiritual traditions. Thus some of the concepts and symbols of the Shekinah and the Kabbalah may be found in alchemy, Hermeticism, mystical Christianity, Freemasonry, Rosicrucianism, the grimoires, modern Pagan traditions and all their many derivatives, as well as the traditions of the magical Qabalah and Christian Cabalah which derived from the Kabbalah.

The study and practise of the Qabalah has largely become focused around the glyph known as *Otz Chiim* – the *'Tree of Life'*. The image of the Qabalistic Tree of Life comprises the ten Sephiroth (*'emanations'*), represented by circles, which are connected by twenty-two horizontal, vertical and diagonal paths. This glyph connects ten, (the number base used my most cultures), with twenty-two, the number of letters in the Hebrew alphabet. The twenty-two also combines the three elements (air, fire and water, without earth which is taken as implicit), the seven classical planets, and the twelve zodiacal signs.

---

209 Haggigah 12a, 70 CE.

The Qabalah is largely based around the process of manifestation and realisation. Manifestation occurs down the Tree of Life, from the most subtle and intangible forces of the pure divine energy to the physical realm. Realisation occurs up the Tree of Life, with insights gained through the unification of the self by journeying towards the divine source. The Shekinah is present at both ends of the Tree of Life, and is inherent to both processes. She is not only the divine wisdom and source of souls which engenders and inspires, but also the tangible presence of the anima mundi.

The first known depiction of the Tree of Life comes from 1516 CE, on the cover of the book *Portae Lucis* (*'Gates of Light'*) by Paul Riccius, a Jew who converted to Christianity. This book contained Latin translations of the Hebrew work *Shaare Orah* (which also means *Gates of Light*) by Rabbi Joseph Gikatilla (1248-1323 CE). The cover is one of the most famous Qabalistic images, showing an old man holding a Tree of Life.

The pattern of the paths of the Tree of Life has varied over the centuries, resulting in different versions being used by Jewish Kabbalists and non-Jewish Cabalists and Qabalists. Likewise the attributions of some symbols like parts of the physical human body have also changed over the centuries.

Of course the tree of life was the sacred symbol of the goddess Asherah, and carved trees or poles to her were placed next to altars to represent the divine polarity of goddess and god, with the altar being to the god who was her consort at the time. This depended on who the dominant god in the area was, and which culture was in power. The tree of life of Asherah may have been the precursor of the Qabalistic Tree of Life, as the menorah candlestick which can be seen as a Kabbalistic prototype may have originally been a stylised version of the Tree of Life in nature.

The idea of a Sacred Tree, or World Tree, i.e. Tree of Life, was found in religion and artwork with appropriate cultural depictions throughout the ancient world. The Sacred Tree is seen in ancient Mesopotamia/Sumer by the fourth millennium BCE, and by the second millennium BCE it occurred in ancient Egypt, Greece and the Harappan Culture of the Indus Valley, which would give rise to the Indian gods. The Tree of Life was often associated with goddesses, such as the Sumerian Inanna, the Egyptian Hathor, and the Canaanite Asherah and would subsequently find expression in later religions and spiritualities such as Buddhism, Christianity, Islam, Judaism and Kabbalah, and even the Norse world tree Yggdrasil, and the world tree found in many indigenous cultures.

The Qabalistic Tree of Life is often described as an apple tree (or pomegranate or other fruit tree), with the Sephiroth representing the apples (or other fruit). In fact the ten Sephiroth (*'emanations'*) are seen as representing the stages of manifestation of the divine creative essence, from its first undivided presence to its physical expression as the planet Earth.

The ten Sephiroth all correspond to a vast range of symbols, from colours to numbers, from planets to plants, from scents to crystals to parts of the human body. Because of these symbolic associations, the Qabalistic Tree of Life is used as a tool for cross-referencing myths, pantheons, cosmologies and philosophies.

# The Four Worlds of the Tree of Life

The Tree of Life is described as manifesting through Four Worlds, called Atziluth (the Archetypal World), Briah (the Creative World), Yetzirah (the Formative World) and Assiah (the Making World). These Worlds take their name from a verse in *Isaiah* which reads, *"Everyone who is called by my name* [Atziluth], *whom I created* [Briah] *for my glory, whom I formed* [Yetzirah] *and made* [Assiah]."[210] It is also interesting to note the word Kavod (*'glory'*) in this sentence, bringing in the influence of the Shekinah, as Kavod is another word used for her.

The Worlds represent the process of manifestation from idea or concept to physical reality. On one level, each Sephira is said to exist in all Four Worlds, which correspond to its Divine Name, archangel, order of angels and heaven, representing different levels of manifestation of the creative essence. Yet on another level the Four Worlds divide the Sephiroth into triads down the Tree of Life based on the principle of force and form balanced in action or repose, with each World containing three of the Sephiroth (with the fourth World only containing the final Sephiroth of Malkuth, which equates to the Earthly Shekinah).

The divine name represents the pure creative essence or divine impulse of a Sephira, the archangel is the lens through which that energy is focused and directed, the order of angels are the forces which enact the manifestation of the divine energy, and the heaven is the receptacle of the divine energy. Thus each of these manifestations represents the creative divine essence at a different level.

The direction of travel through the Worlds of the Tree of Life determines the nature of the result. Divine energy manifests down the Tree and understanding and wisdom are realised through experience moving up the Tree.

| World | Atziluth | Briah | Yetzirah | Assiah |
|---|---|---|---|---|
| Action | Emanating | Creating | Forming | Making |
| Process | Intent | Concept | Realisation | Manifestation |
| Divinity | Divine Name | Archangel | Order of Angels | Heaven |
| Tetragrammaton | Yod | Heh | Vav | Heh (final) |
| Divine Face | Father | Mother - Heavenly Shekinah | Son | Daughter - Earthly Shekinah |
| Element | Fire | Water | Air | Earth |
| Contains the Sephiroth | Kether Chokmah Binah | Chesed Geburah Tiphereth | Netzach Hod Yesod | Malkuth |

210 Isaiah 43:7, C7th-C6th BCE.

# The Shekinah in Qabalistic Symbolism

Within the divine fourfold name of Tetragrammaton (IHVH - Yod-Heh-Vav-Heh, pronounced Yahweh or Yahveh) we see the feminine influence of the Shekinah being expressed first as the mother who is the Understanding of Binah (the first Heh) and then through physical manifestation as the daughter of Malkuth (the final Heh). Heh is sometimes used as a symbol for the united soul, having the numeration of five, which is also the number of parts of the soul.

The energy of Creation that is the initial manifestation of the Greater Shekinah, i.e. the World of Briah containing Binah (Understanding), is manifested in Malkuth through the daughter as the World of Assiah, or Making, also known as the Lesser or Exiled Shekinah. Malkuth represents the making of the creative ideas, the reification of the generative principle in nature; hence nature, the Earth and indeed the Garden of Eden are all referred to as feminine in Qabalah.

The classic medieval Kabbalistic text, the *Bahir* contains many references to the daughter, matron, princess or wife in tales, and these usually refer to the Shekinah through symbolic comparisons or parables. One parable describes how the whole Tree of Life embodies the Shekinah, and how she is the path to divine union (note the thirty-two paths indicating this connection):

> *"These are the 32 paths. This is like a king who was in the innermost chamber of his palace, and the number of room was 32, and there was a path to every chamber. Did it suit the king to allow everyone to enter his chambers by these paths? No! But did it suit him not to display openly his pearls and hidden treasures, jewelled settings and beautiful things at all? No! What did the king do? He took his daughter and concentrated all paths in her and*

*in her garments, and whoever wishes to enter
the interior must look this way at her."211*

A version of the *Book of 3 Enoch* hints at the
association between the Shekinah and the Tree of Life. The
nine different gates mentioned could imply the Sephiroth of
the Tree of Life, with God being the first Sephira, Kether. In
his description, Enoch says:

> *"After one hour the Holy One, blessed be He,
> opened to me the gates of Shekinah, gates of
> wisdom, gates of peace, gates of strength, gates
> of might, gates of speech, gates of song, gates of
> Qedushah [prayer], gates of chant."212*

The most blatant Biblical reference to the proto-
Shekinah may be found as the Wisdom Goddess in the
third century BCE *Book of Proverbs*, 8:1-12. This book is
one of the great pieces of wisdom literature on the divine
feminine, with astonishingly clear content and despite its
pre-Kabbalistic date it contains a very strong flavour of
Kabbalistic symbolism. The wording is very reminiscent of
the philosophy associated with the Egyptian goddess of
truth and balance, Ma'at, discussed earlier as a predecessor
of some of the concepts expressed by the Shekinah in the
Kabbalah.

> *"1. Does not wisdom call, and does not
> understanding raise her voice?
> 2. On the heights, beside the way, at the
> crossroads she takes her stand;
> 3. Beside the gates in front of the town, at the
> entrance of the portals she cries out:
> 4. 'To you, O people, I call, and my cry is to all
> that live.
> 5. O simple ones, learn prudence; acquire
> intelligence, you who lack it.*

---

211 Bahir, 36, C12th CE.
212 MS Florence Plut 44.13, N.D.

*6. Hear, for I will speak noble things, and from my lips will come what is right;*
*7. for my mouth will utter truth; wickedness is an abomination to my lips.*
*8. All the words of my mouth are righteous; there is nothing twisted or crooked in them.*
*9. They are all straight to one who understands and right to those who find knowledge.*
*10. Take my instruction instead of silver, and knowledge rather than choice gold;*
*11. for wisdom is better than jewels, and all that you may desire cannot compare with her.*
*12. I, wisdom, live with prudence, and I attain knowledge and discretion."*

This chapter goes on to describe how the Wisdom Goddess existed before creation (*Proverbs 8:22-31*), being the first act of the divine impulse. The next chapter, *Proverbs 9*, begins with a verse which alludes to the doctrine of the Seven Palaces, referring to seven pillars, corresponding to the seven classical planets and the seven lower Sephiroth on the Tree of Life.

*"Wisdom has built her house, she has hewn her seven pillars ..."*[213]

The seven pillars correspond to the seven palaces or lower Sephiroth traversed by the Merkavah rider in his quest for the glory of the divine presence in Merkavah Mysticism.

As well as the Shekinah sitting radiating glory on a throne, there are also numerous descriptions in Merkavah Mysticism of her splendour and glory shining on the faces of some of the highest angels, and being too bright for other angels to look at, emphasising her holiness. This theme was developed by early Kabbalists like Judah ben Barzillai

---

213 Proverbs 9:1, C3rd BCE.

(eleventh century CE) who emphasised that the Shekinah was the great light of God's glory.

The word *kavod* (*'glory'*, KBD) is often equated with the Shekinah, so when it occurs, substituting the word Shekinah gives a range of appropriate symbols and philosophies being expressed. E.g. *"The whole world is full of his glory"*[214] is describing the common theme of the universality of the Shekinah as the world soul. The precedent for this is seen in some Jewish texts which interpreted biblical verses as portrayals of the Shekinah. Thus the Abot de R. Nathan interprets the phrase *"and the earth shone with His glory"*[215] as *"This is the face of Shekinah"*.

The literature of Merkavah mysticism also reveals similar themes, describing God and the Shekinah as *"He who is exalted with chains of crowns, encircled by branches of brilliance, Who covers the heavens with the branch of his Glory [i.e. Shekinah]."*[216]

That the numbers attributed to the letters in *Kavod* (KBVD) should add to thirty-two, the same as the numeration for *Lev* (*'heart'*, LB), and the number of paths on the Tree of Life, is a central theme in Kabbalah and its derivatives of Qabalah and Cabalah.

---

214 Isaiah 6:3, C7th-C6th BCE.
215 Ezekiel 43:2, C6th BCE).
216 Synopse 253, Hekhalot Rabbati, C3rd-C7th CE.

# The Sephiroth

In the *Zohar*, symbolic reference is made to the Tree of Life as the Shekinah, with the words:

> *"There are ten curtains, which are ten expanses. And who are they? The curtains of the Dwelling, which are ten and are susceptible to knowing by the wise of heart."*[217]

This passage is describing the ten Sephiroth (as curtains or expanses), which comprise the Shekinah as the Tree of Life (Dwelling). The wise of heart hints at both the Shekinah (wisdom) and also the Tree of Life itself, as the numbers attributed to the letters of heart (Lev) adds up to thirty-two, the number of paths and Sephiroth of the Tree of Life. To explore the Tree of Life in association with the Shekinah, we need to consider each of the Sephiroth in turn.

# Kether

Kether (*'Crown'*) is the first Sephira on the Tree of Life, and represents the divine essence in its first manifestation from the unmanifest and limitless veils of negativity. It is attributed to the first swirlings (*Rashith haGilgalim*) of creation, hence it has the divine name of Eheieh (AHIH), meaning *'I Am'*, representing the self awareness of the primordial divinity.

Another divine name attributed to Kether is Elion (*'Most High'*), which is derived from the Phoenician creator god Elioun or Elyon. The Greek version of this name is Hypsistos, which subsequently manifested as Theos

---

217 Zohar 2:165a, C13th CE.

Hypsistos (*'Highest God'*), whose cult spread amongst Jews, Christians and Pagans around the Mediterranean during the second century BCE and persisted for several centuries. This cult may well have been a significant influence on the development of the early Kabbalah or even on some Gnostic ideas, as hinted at by the following oracular inscription (dated to the second century BCE) found at Oenoanda in Northern Lycia (modern Turkey):

> *"Born of itself, untaught, without a mother, unshakeable, not contained in a name, known by many names, dwelling in fire, this is god. We, his angels, are a small part of god."*[218]

Kether is considered unknowable, and hence the attribution of the archangel Metatron (*'He who serves behind the Throne'*) as the voice of the unknowable God here. Metatron is particularly associated with the Heavenly Shekinah as her agent, giving an example of the connection between the divine source and divine wisdom. The order of angels called Holy Living Creatures (*Chaioth HaQadosh*) are attributed to Kether.

# Chokmah

Chokmah (*'Wisdom'*) is the second Sephira on the Tree of Life, and represents the zodiac (*Masloth*), the stars which form the outer limits of our perception of the universe. It has the divine name of Yah (IH) attributed to it, which is comprised of the masculine letter Yod and feminine letter Heh. These letters combine to form the first half of Tetragrammaton (IHVH), and are known as the Inner Chamber, representing as they do the implied hieros gamos (divine marriage).

---

218 The Cult of Theos Hypsistos between Pagans, Jews, and Christians, Mitchell, 1999:81-148.

Chokmah emphasises the dual nature of wisdom, for although it is considered at times to represent the divine masculine, and heads the White Masculine Pillar of Mercy on the Tree of Life, it can also be feminine, and represent the wisdom of the Heavenly Shekinah, seen in the stars of the night sky. Raziel (*'Herald of God'*), the archangel of wisdom, is appropriately attributed here, and the order of angels is the Wheels (*'Ophanim'*).

# Binah

Binah (*'Understanding'*) is the third Sephira on the Tree of Life, and represents the planet Saturn (*Shabathai*), the outermost of the seven classical planets. It has the divine name of Yahweh (IHVH) attributed to it, the Tetragrammaton which is a central part of the Qabalah, and emphasises the importance of this Sephira. Yahweh was originally a Canaanite god, like El, who became incorporated into the Qabalah and became the god of Judaism and the *Old Testament*.

Binah is particularly associated with the Heavenly or Greater Shekinah, and is at the top of the Black or Feminine Pillar of Severity on the Tree of Life. The order of angels is the Aralim (*'Strong and Mighty Ones'*), and they are ruled by the archangel Zaphkiel (*'Beholder of God'*). The presence of the Shekinah (divine wisdom) here is indicated in the *Thirty-Two Paths of Wisdom*, in the words:

> *"The Third Intelligence is called the Sanctifying Intelligence, the Foundation of Primordial Wisdom."*[219]

There is a strong relationship between the tenth Sephira of Malkuth as the physical realm of the elements, with Binah, the Sephira which represents the beginnings of

---

[219] The Thirty-Two Paths of Wisdom, C11th CE.

form. When Malkuth is described as *"sitting on the Throne of Binah"*,[220] it highlights this relationship. The Throne is a title of Binah, and demonstrates the power of Saturn as the highest manifestation of the element of Earth to give solidity and form. It also emphasises the divine vision of Ezekiel of the throne of God, and hints at the Egyptian goddess Isis, whose name means Throne, and who shares many qualities with Binah.

# Daath

Daath (*'Knowledge'*) is a paradox, being a Sephira that isn't. The Kabbalistic texts are very clear about there being ten Sephiroth, *"ten and not nine, ten and not eleven"*,[221] states the *Sepher Yetzirah*. Yet Daath plays a significant role on the Tree of Life, being the gateway between the pure divine force of the Supernal Triad, and the manifesting form of the seven Sephiroth below.

The best way to describe Daath is perhaps as a liminal point on the Tree of Life which has some of the characteristics of a Sephira. Daath is particularly connected with the Sephiroth of Chokmah and Binah, as seen in the verse from *Proverbs* which is seen in the Kabbalah as clarifying the role of Daath as a gateway:

> *"The Lord by wisdom [Chokmah] founded the earth; by understanding [Binah] he established the heavens; by his knowledge [Daath] the deeps broke open, and the clouds drop down the dew."*[222]

A significant symbolism associated with Daath is also that of sexual union, which can be seen here in the clouds

---

220 The Thirty-Two Paths of Wisdom, C11th CE.
221 Sepher Yetzirah 1:4, C2nd CE.
222 Proverbs 3:19-20, C3rd BCE.

dropping dew. In this context knowledge is equated to the sexual act in the Biblical phrase *"and he knew his wife"*. Thus Daath can be seen as the Hieros Gamos or sacred marriage of the divine father and mother, Chokmah and Binah, which is why one of its titles is the Bridal Chamber.

Because Daath is and is not a Sephira, it does not have manifestations through the Four Worlds in the same way. There is no order of angels or heaven associated with Daath. However, the divine name Ruach HaQadosh (*Spirit of Holiness*) is appropriate for Daath, connecting it again to the Shekinah, and descriptions of the archangel Anphiel (*'Foliage of God'*) in the early *Hekhalot* texts make it clear he too fits with Daath.[223]

Daath is particularly associated with prophecy, being attributed to the throat on the human body. The connection between Daath and prophecy as the words of the Shekinah was implied in the rites of the Fellowship of the Rose Cross, as may be seen in the words spoken by the priestess in the initiation for the grade of Adeptus Exemptus:

> *"Daath is the Ark of the Eternal Covenant. The hope of the height is the hope of ascension therein. It is indeed the World of Ascension, wherein is a living stillness. It is the place of the Word in its fullness, an undifferentiated deep of being, withdrawn in the Supernals forever. But as it withdraws inwardly so also it sets forth toward utterance, and from the Word in Daath flow down those symbols which are thought and speech at the highest."*[224]

---

223 For a discussion of this see Practical Qabalah Magick, Rankine & d'Este, 2009:104-106.
224 Adeptus Exemptus Ceremony, Fellowship of the Rosy Cross, 1916:37-38.

# Chesed

Chesed (*'Mercy'*) is the fourth Sephira on the Tree of Life, representing the planet of Jupiter (*Tzedeq*) and is also commonly known as Gedulah (*'Glory'*). Chesed is the first reflection of Chokmah, and represents the highest level that form can take before being transmuted to pure force. Chesed is linked with the highest aspects of water, which can be seen as the force that overcomes all.

With its alternative name of Glory, Chesed recalls the Kavod (*'Glory'*) which is the manifestation of the Shekinah. The divine name of Chesed is El (AL), which was taken from the name of the supreme god of the Canaanite pantheon who was the husband of the goddess Asherah, who influenced the Shekinah.

Chesed is a place of reconciliation, of ensuring that previous experience is integrated and balanced to move forward and manifest the higher wisdom it reflects. This is emphasised by the fourfold nature of Chesed, with four being a number of balance, and its importance is seen through its manifestation as the fourfold name (Tetragrammaton), the four elements and the Four Worlds. Hence Chesed is described in the *Thirty-Two Paths of Wisdom* as *"containing all the holy powers."*[225] The archangel of Chesed is Zadkiel (*'Righteousness of God'*), who rules the order of angels called the Chasmalim (*'Brilliant Ones'*).

# Geburah

Geburah (*'Strength'* or *'Power'*) is the fifth Sephira on the Tree of Life, representing the planet Mars (*Madim*) and is also commonly known as Pachad (*'Fear'*) and Din

---

225 The Thirty-Two Paths of Wisdom, C11th CE.

('*Justice*'). The *Thirty-Two Paths of Wisdom* said of Geburah that:

> "*The Fifth Path is called the Radical Intelligence because it resembles Unity, uniting itself to Binah, Understanding, which emanates from the primordial depths of Chokmah, Wisdom.*"[226]

In the thirteenth century CE Kabbalistic text, *Treatise on the Left Emanation*, it is hinted at that all evil comes from Samael in the realm of Geburah, the fiery unbalanced power of Mars. When it is balanced it becomes the '*power and the glory*' (Geburah and Gedulah). So how does it resemble unity? The answer to this lies in the number five, which is the numeration of the Hebrew letter Heh, which symbolises the Shekinah in the Tetragrammaton, and also is a motif of the soul, which has five parts when the higher aspects are considered.

The divine name of Geburah is Elohim Gibor ('*the Strong Gods*'), emphasising the power of this Sephira. The archangel of Geburah is Khamael ('*He who sees God*') or Samael, who was said to be the husband of the Greater Lilith. The order of angels is the Seraphim ('*Fiery Serpents*').

# Tiphereth

Tiphereth ('*Beauty*') is the sixth Sephira on the Tree of Life, representing the Sun (*Shamash*), and was also previously known as Rachamin ('*Compassion*'). Tiphereth is in the centre of the Tree of Life, connected to all the other Sephiroth except only Malkuth, its bride. It has a number of titles including Husband and Blessed Holy One (*Ha-Qadosh Barukh Hu*), both referring to its relationship to the Bride (the Sephira of Malkuth), and the Lesser Countenance

---

226 The Thirty-Two Paths of Wisdom, C11th CE.

(*Zair Anpin*) referring to its relationship to the Greater Countenance (*Arik Anpin*) of Kether.

Tiphereth is the lower reflection of the unknowable divine that is Kether, hence its title of the Reflecting Mirror. It represents the divine child, and may thus be seen as the point of illumination, the product of Wisdom (Chokmah) and Understanding (Binah).

The role of Tiphereth is to engender growth and evolution through its illuminating energy. Tiphereth is the point of balance between the directed forces of the upper Tree and their resulting forms in the lower Tree. The higher energies of the Tree find their expression through the centre, and those energies manifest into forms lower down on the Tree.

The divine name of Tiphereth is Eloah, which combines the name El with the VH (Vav Heh) that is the second half of Tetragrammaton. The archangel of Tiphereth is Michael (*'He who is like God'*), and he rules the order of angels called the Malachim (*'Kings'*).

# Netzach

Netzach (*'Victory'* or *'Firmness'*) is the seventh Sephira on the Tree of Life, representing the planet Venus (*Nogah*). Nogah is also the amber glow seen in the vision of Ezekiel and equated to the *'speaking silence'* (*Chasmal*) experienced during meditation when the inner dialogue is silent.

Amongst its titles are Confidence (*Bitachon*) and Eternity, which emphasise the powerful nature of this Sephira. Although Netzach sits at the bottom of the masculine Pillar of Mercy, as the Sephira of Venus it is by nature more feminine.

The divine name of Netzach is Yahweh Sabaoth (*Lord of Hosts*), the latter name (Sabaoth, pronounced *Zavaot*) being frequently used as a divine name of power by itself in Greek charms, as seen in the *Greek Magical Papyri* and as the name of oen of the archons in Gnostic texts. The archangel of Netzach is Uriel (*'the Light of God'*), and he rules the order of angels called the Elohim (*'Gods'*), which is derived from the Canaanite term and also found in some Gnostic texts such as the *Book of Baruch* as a name for God.

# Hod

Hod (*'Splendour'*) is the eighth Sephira on the Tree of Life, representing the planet Mercury (*Kohkav*). Mercury is traditionally associated with the intellect and the memory and knowledge. The *Thirty-Two Paths of Wisdom* emphasises a connection between Hod and Gedulah (Glory, another name for Chesed), which also brings the Shekinah to mind due to the connection between Glory and her:

> *"The Eighth Path is called the Absolute or Perfect Intelligence because it is the mean of the Primordial, which has no root by which it can cleave or rest, save in the hidden places of Gedulah, from which emanates its proper essence."*[227]

The divine name of this Sephira is Elohim Sabaoth (*Gods of Hosts*), emphasising its polarity with Netzach, which also has Sabaoth in its divine name. The archangel is Raphael (*'the Healer of God'*), who rules over the order of angels called the Bene Elohim (*'Sons of Gods'*).

The Bene Elohim were derived from the Canaanite Sons of El and Athirat (Asherah), who were a group of seventy gods. They became demoted in the *Old Testament* to an order of angels who appear in several of the books, having been variously the Bene Elohim (*'Sons of Gods'*), Bene haElohim (*'Sons of God'*) and Bene Elion (*'Sons of the*

---

227 The Thirty-Two Paths of Wisdom, C11th CE.

*most High*).[228]   Modern Biblical texts commonly translate these as *'heavenly beings'* or *'holy ones'*.

# Yesod

Yesod (*'Foundation'*) is the ninth Sephira on the Tree of Life, representing the classical planet of the Moon (*Levanah*).   This recalls the Shekinah as the foundation stone of the temple, and that Yesod is attributed to the sexual organs, and hence particularly associated with the sexual act. Its position between Tiphereth and Malkuth on the Tree of Life emphasises this function, with Yesod symbolising the hieros gamos between the Sun and Earth, God (the son) and the Earthly Shekinah (Malkuth).

The divine name of Yesod is Shaddai (ShDI) meaning *'Almighty'*.   The original source of this word is unknown, however there is a strong argument that the meaning of this word may be derived from the Hebrew word *šad*, meaning *'breast'*, giving a meaning of *'One of the Breast'*.[229]   This would fit with one of Asherah's titles as *'One of the Womb'*, emphasising her role as a nurturing fertility goddess.

The archangel of Yesod is Gabriel (*'The Strength of God'*), and he rules over the order of angels called Cherubim or Kerubim (*'the Strong Ones'*), who are particularly associated with the Shekinah, as discussed in the later chapter *Mother of Angels*.

# Malkuth

Malkuth (*'Kingdom'*) is the tenth Sephira on the Tree of Life, representing the Four Elements of Air, Earth, Fire and

---

228 Genesis 6:2, 6:4 (C10th-C8th BCE); Job 1:6, 38:7 (C3rd BCE); Psalms 29:1, 82:6, 89:7 (C10th-C2nd BCE).
229 Shadday as a Goddess Epithet, Lutzky, 1998:15-36.

Water, and is also sometimes called Shekinah in early Kabbalistic texts.

Malkuth is the only Sephira that is not part of a triad, though it is linked to the three Sephiroth of the Astral Triad (Yesod, Hod and Netzach). Malkuth is said to receive the energies of all the other emanations of the Tree. This is why so many of the titles of Malkuth describe it as a Gate, for it is the Gate to the rest of the Tree of Life, i.e. both the actualisation of the self as the inner Tree, and to other realms as symbolised by the Sephiroth and Worlds.

The connection between the Shekinah and Malkuth as the tenth Sephira is also hinted at in the *Sanhedrin* texts, when the Roman emperor taunted Rabbi Gamaliel about that fact that the Shekinah rests upon every gathering of ten people.[230]

Another clear indication is to be found in the Gematria of the word Shekinah. Gematria is the Qabalistic technique which makes use of the fact that every letter in the Hebrew alphabet has a numerical attribution. By adding together the numerical values of the letters in a word you produce a word total. This word total is then compared to other words which sum to the same total to make connections between their meanings. The total for Shekinah (ShKINH) is 385, the same as the total for Assiah (OShIH), so it can be said that Shekinah equates to the World of Assiah.

This is expressed by the thirteenth century Kabbalist David ben Judah Hehasid, who wrote of the Shekinah and her qualities in his work *Sepher Mar'ot Hazove'ot*:

> *"Malkhut, who is called Sod Ha'efshar, the Secret of the Possible. Thus, She gives birth to whatever She wants to bring down to the world. Therefore it says, 'for you do not know what a day may bring forth'"*[231]

---

230 Sanhedrin 39b, c. 100 CE.
231 David ben Yehudah Hehasid and his Book of Mirrors, Matt, 1980:165.

The divine name of Malkuth is Adonai (ADNI), meaning *'Lord'*. In Judaism Adonai is used as a substitute for Tetragrammaton, for Yahweh is never pronounced. The archangel is Sandalphon (*'Brotherly One'*), who rules over the order of angels called the Ashim (*'Flames'*).

| # | Name | Divine Name | Archangel | Order of Angels | Heaven |
|---|------|-------------|-----------|-----------------|--------|
| 1 | Kether | AHIH (Eheieh) | Metatron | Chaioth HaQadosh | Rashith haGilgalim |
| 2 | Chokmah | IH (Yah) | Raziel | Ophanim | Masloth |
| 3 | Binah | IHVH (Yahveh) | Zaphkiel | Aralim | Shabathai |
| 4 | Chesed | Al (El) | Zadkiel | Chasmalim | Tzedeq |
| 5 | Geburah | ALHIM GIBVR (Elohim Givor) | Khamael | Seraphim | Madim |
| 6 | Tiphereth | ALVH (Eloah) | Michael | Malachim | Shamash |
| 7 | Netzach | IHVH TzBAVTh (Yahveh Tzavaot) | Uriel | Elohim | Nogah |
| 8 | Hod | ALHIM TzBAVTh (Elohim Tzavaot) | Raphael | Bene Elohim | Kohkav |
| 9 | Yesod | ShDI (Shaddai) | Gabriel | Cherubim | Levanah |
| 10 | Malkuth | ADNI (Adonai) | Sandalphon | Ashim | Cholim Yesodoth |
| 11 | Daath | RVACh HQDOSh (Ruach HaQadosh) | Anphiel | - | - |

The different connections between the Shekinah and the individual Sephiroth express the intimate connection between the Kabbalah/Qabalah and the Shekinah. This is found throughout Kabbalistic teachings and their more modern Qabalistic derivatives, and demonstrates the emphasis in these teachings on the divine as being both feminine and masculine.

# Creation & the Created

This chapter explores creation myths particularly associated with the Shekinah in Kabbalistic teachings. Additionally the differences in perspective found in Kabbalistic viewpoints and their relevance to the Shekinah are considered further. Finally we touch on medieval Kabbalistic descriptions of how to visualise the Shekinah during the sexual act, showing again how the Shekinah is associated with the creation process.

## A Kabbalistic Creation Myth

Tzim-Tzum, or Zim-Zum (meaning *'contraction'* or *'constriction'*), describes the concept of the original undivided limitlessness (the *Ain Soph*) contracting to form a *'space'* into which all of creation could and would manifest (i.e. the Four Worlds comprising the Sephiroth of the Tree of Life, with all its levels and beings, from angels to humans to plants). The presence of the divine was considered to still permeate the space, but the dynamic essence had withdrawn. A good analogy of this is a beautiful perfume lingering in a room, the woman who wore the perfume may have left the room, but her presence and the knowledge she was there echoes in the fragrance she left behind.

The *Zohar* (1.15a) describes this process:

> *"In the beginning of the King's authority*
> *The Lamp of Darkness*
> *Engraved a hollow in the Supernal*
> *Luminescence*
> *And there emerged out of the Hidden of Hidden*
> *The Mystery of the Infinite*
> *An unformed line, imbedded in a ring*
> *Measured with a thread."*

This could be viewed like a grain of sand in an oyster, which accretes layers and forms a beautiful pearl. The sand grain is the space within the Ain Soph. This creation of space is the preparation for creation, and is the first instance of separation, where the divine moves from immanence to transcendence in the prepared space.

However the initial separation allowed for a disharmony through lack of unity. The light of God, i.e. the Shekinah, entered the empty vessels of the Sephiroth, of which all but the upper three broke, as they were unable to hold the divine emanations. This *'breaking of the vessels'* (*shevirah*) as it is known, resulted in the shards falling into the prepared space and taking sparks of the divine light with them. Most of the divine light returned to the Ain Soph, apart from these sparks.

There is a Kabbalistic teaching that the ten original Sephiroth became reconstituted as five *Parzufim* (*faces*) when the divine *'breaking of the vessels'* took place. The five Parzufim can be attributed to the Sephiroth of the second perfect Tree of Life which was formed with the capacity for all of the Sephiroth to give and receive, thus ensuring they would not break.

The Parzufim correspond to the five letters of Elohim (ALHIM), the divine name which means *'Gods'* and is found throughout the *Old Testament* (and in earlier Canaanite myths and subsequent Gnostic myths), and to Tetragrammaton (IHVH), considered the ultimate name of the divine. They are as follows:

| Parzufim | Face | Sephiroth | Part of IHVH | Part of ALHIM |
|---|---|---|---|---|
| Arik Anpin | Greater Countenance | Kether | Point of the Yod | Aleph |
| Aba | Father | Chokmah | Yod | Lamed |
| Aima | Mother | Binah | Heh | Heh |
| Zair Anpin | Lesser Countenance or Son | Chesed – Yesod | Vav | Yod |
| Nukya | Daughter | Malkuth | Heh (final) | Mem |

This idea teaches that the lower Sephiroth (below Daath) of the primeval Tree of Life could only receive the divine emanations from above, but could not interact or give. As a result of this they were overwhelmed and shattered, causing the *'Breaking of the Vessels'*. This is referred to symbolically in *Genesis 36:32-39* describing the seven Kings of Edom, who are considered a symbolic allegory for the seven lower Sephiroth.

The broken pieces of these vessels fell to Assiah, the lowest of the Four Worlds, which is the physical plane. The ten Sephiroth were then created anew in a more perfect form where they could interact, giving the Tree of Life. The broken pieces of the original Tree are considered to be the sparks of divine light which infused all life. This divine light was from the Shekinah, which is how we all came to bear a spark of her divinity within us.

The broken [pieces of the original Tree of Life are also considered to have formed the Qliphoth (*'shells'*), which can challenge but cannot give, and need to be overcome to gain an understanding of the true nature of each of the Sephiroth.

The *'breaking of the vessels'* can be interpreted from two different perspectives - optimistic and pessimistic. The optimistic view is that this event was the birth of the universe, with all the pain and difficulties we as humans have come to expect from birth, but on a universal scale. The pessimistic view is that the universes slipped, and Assiah (the physical world) is now in the World of Shells, and to restore it all the sparks of light trapped in this realm must be freed. This doctrine is called *'restoration'* (*tikkun*), and can be seen as restoring the divine spark within everything to the Shekinah, where it originated.

An earlier version of this doctrine is implied by the *Chaldean Oracles of Zoroaster*, which includes a description from the philosopher Porphyry, who stated:

> *"There is above the Celestial Lights an Incorruptible Flame always sparkling; the Spring of Life, the Formation of all Beings, the Original of all things! This Flame produceth all things, and nothing perisheth but what it consumeth. It maketh Itself known by Itself. This Fire cannot be contained in any Place, it is without Body and without Matter. It encompasseth the Heavens. And there goeth out from it little Sparks, which make all the Fires of the Sun, of the Moon, and of the Stars."*[232]

# The Five Adams

Some of the early Kabbalistic texts talk about Adam Kadmon (or Qadmon), who is also called the Primordial Man. To understand the concept of Adam Kadmon it is important to realise that the Adam who was expelled from Eden with Eve was actually the fourth of the Adams.

The first Adam was Adam Kadmon, the primordial human, who was viewed as the fifth World, above Atziluth, containing the potential of the other four Worlds within him. This fifth World is actually another name for the Ain Soph, or veil of limitlessness, and was described as being the dwelling place of Tetragrammaton, the unpronounceable name. It is sometimes equated with the dot on the Yod of the unpronounceable name, Tetragrammaton, as the first impulse of the ultimate.

---

232 Chaldean Oracles of Zoroaster, Westcott, 1895:53.

Adam Kadmon was formed by a single beam of light (which was a manifestation of the Shekinah) sent forth from the Ain Soph (*Limitlessness*), which burst forth from his eyes, ears, nose and mouth as the lights of the Sephiroth (these facial orifices are also known as the seven gates of the soul) of the Tree of Life.

The light from the eyes filled the vessels of light that were the Supernal Triad of the Sephiroth of Kether, Chokmah and Binah. However when the light filled the vessels of the lower Sephiroth it was so intense that the vessels broke. This was the *'Breaking of the Vessels'* (*Shevirah*). The primordial light also equates to the *"Let there be light"*[233] of the *Book of Genesis*.

Some sources consider Adam Kadmon to have been the first template of divine manifestation, the *'first Adam'*, reflected through the Four Worlds in different manifestations. This is part of the doctrine known as the *'Five Adams'*.

The second Adam is the one described in *Genesis 1:27*, *"God created man with His image. In the image of God, He created him; male and female He created them."* This Adam is the Atzilutic Adam, or *'Adam of light'*. A significant word here is *'them'*, implying that this Adam was one of many, not a single being, and also that *'male and female created He them'* showing the presence of both genders, and not that of the male as being first which is often assumed.

The third Adam is the described one in *Genesis 2:7*, *"God formed man out of the dust of the ground, and breathed into his nostrils a breath of life. Man became a living soul."* This Adam is the Briatic Adam, or the *'Adam of dust'*, who names all the creatures (*Genesis 2:19-20*). The *Zohar* specifically brings the Shekinah in to this stage, emphasising the divine polarity involved in creating life. It said:

---

233 Genesis 1:3, C10th-C8th BCE.

> *"'And the Lord God formed the man out of dust from the earth and breathed into his nostrils or soul the breath of life,' the divine Shekinah. Man is a threefold product of life (Nephesh), spirit (Ruach), and soul (Neshamah), by the blending and union of which he became a living spirit, a manifestation of the Divine."*[234]

The fourth Adam is the one from whom Eve is created in *Genesis 2:21-23*, created by the process of separation undergone by the third Adam. The original word is actually *'side'* not *'rib'*, as was explained in the *Zohar*, which implies that the third Adam was a hermaphrodite who contained both male and female. Indeed this is back up by lines in Genesis such as, *"closed the flesh"* (2:21) and *"bone from my bones, and flesh from my flesh"* (2:23). This Adam is the Yetziric Adam, and was said to be the first of all human souls, having received the divine influence of the Shekinah.

The fifth Adam is the one who has been expelled from the Garden of Eden (*Genesis 3:23-24*). This Adam is the Assiatic Adam, who seeks to return to a state of grace.

# All in the Perspective

We know that the Shekinah is seen as wisdom, and yet the second Sephira of the Tree of Life *Chokmah* (Wisdom) is usually viewed as being masculine. However this is entirely relative to how its position is interpreted on the Tree of Life. Each Sephira is viewed as being negative to the one above it and positive to the one below, so is it also the case that each Sephira is feminine to the one above it and masculine to the one below. This is expressed in the grimoire *Sepher Raziel*, which stated, *"Of understanding, receive wisdom."* This also means that the tenth Sephira of

---

234 Zohar I.27a, C13th CE.

Malkuth (the Earthly Shekinah) is the only one on the Tree which is wholly female.

Hence although Chokmah is known by titles such as the Father (Aba), this is in respect of its relationship with Binah as the Mother (Ama), not in its relationship to Kether, where it is perceived as feminine (Chokmatha). This is best illustrated in the *Zohar*, which observed this in relation to the letter Heh's attributed to the Shekinah in the Tetragrammaton:

> *"From this nose, from the openings of the nostrils, the Spirit of Life rusheth forth upon Microprosopus. And from that opening of the nose, from those openings of the nostrils, dependeth the letter Heh, in order to establish the other and Inferior Heh. And that Spirit proceedeth from the hidden brain [Kether], and She is called the Spirit of Life, and through that Spirit will all men understand ChKMThA, Chokmatha, Wisdom."*[235]

# Kabbalistic Union

In Kabbalah the divine union of the Lesser Shekinah and God is seen as being expressed through the sunrise every morning, when the rays of the Sun (Tiphereth) shine onto the Earth (Malkuth) and engender life and warmth. However the human expression of this union was written about explicitly by medieval Kabbalists.

The sixteenth century Kabbalist, Rabbi Moses Cordovero (1522-70 CE), who systemised the Kabbalah into the root of what it is now, wrote about the Shekinah and sexual union. His teachings are extremely clear, and perhaps surprisingly graphic in their instructions to husband and wife considering the period they date from.

---

235 Zohar, 5.136-138, C13th CE.

They parallel the practice of a couple identifying with the Hindu goddess Shakti and god Shiva in tantric rites. In a commentary on the *Zohar* he wrote:

> *"Their desire, both his and hers, was to unite Shekinah. He focused on Tiphereth, and his wife on Malkuth. His union was to join Shekinah; she focused correspondingly on being Shekinah and uniting with her husband, Tiphereth."*[236]

Cordovero may have drawn inspiration from the fifteenth century writings of Ephraim Ben Gershon, who in his *Homily to a Groom*, gave very clear instructions for the magical process to be enacted during the sexual act.

> *"Thus do Kabbalists know that thoughts originate in the rational soul, which emanates from the supreme. And thought has the power to strip off and rise and reach its source, and when reaching its source it attains communication with the supernal light from which it came, and both become one. When thought once again stretches down from on high, all becomes one line in the imagination, and the supernal light comes down through the power of thought that draws it down, and the Shekinah is found down below. The clear light then spreads to the thinker's location. So did early priests reach communion with the supremes through thought in order to draw down the supreme light, and all beings would thus grow and multiply and be blessed in accordance with the power of thought."*[237]

The divine marriage is also expressed every week in Judaism, with the Shekinah being the Sabbath Bride and

---

236 Included in Or ha-Hayyim, Azulai, C17th CE.
237 Homilies, Ephraim B. Gershon, C15th CE.

Queen, who is united with God every Friday evening. The *Zohar* emphasises this equation of the Shekinah as Shabbat Bride:

> *"Then this pavilion was sanctified with supernal holiness and adorned with its crowns, finally rising ascendantly in a crown of tranquillity and given a sublime name, a holy name: Sabbath."*[238]

The mistress of the house (who represents the Shekinah) commonly leads the Shabbat ceremonies, lighting the two candles, and everyone turns to face the door to welcome the Shekinah to the feast and sings *Lekha Dodi* (*'Come my beloved'*), an old wedding song based on the erotic divine love song of the *Song of Solomon*.[239] This is also a time when sexual relations between husband and wife are particularly encouraged, as it is a sympathetic re-enactment of the union of God and the Shekinah.

It is clear that teachings about the Shekinah have gained depth and greater perspective over the centuries as the wealth of material produced by great religious and philosophical minds has increased. In the case of the Shekinah these new perspectives are firmly based on older teachings, and expound deep wisdom rather than creating unfounded views without a firm basis.

---

238 Zohar 2:128a, C13th CE.
239 Lines in the song make this relationship clear, e.g. 'Your God will rejoice in you, As a groom rejoices in a bride' (29-30); 'Come in peace, crown of her husband' (35); 'Come O Bride! Come O Bride!' (38).

# Light of Creation

> *"There are lights upon lights, one more clear than another, each one dark by comparison with the one above it from which it receives light. As for the Supreme Cause, all lights are dark in its presence."*
> ~ Zohar 1.23a, C13th CE

Light is a key concept in Qabalah, and as the Shekinah is the primordial light which created the universe, descriptions of light are often associated with her. The association between the Feminine Divine and light is an important one, as Light is usually associated with the concept of giving or emanating and emphasises active creative power, in contrast to vessels which are associated with receptivity or acceptance.

> *"On the fourth day God made the luminaries - sun, moon, and stars - of three substances, air, light, and fire. He took aerial material and prepared vessels like lamps, and mixed fire with light, and filled them."*[240]

Light and lamps (vessels containing light) were extremely important in the worship of Theos Hypsistos ('the

---

240 The Book of the Bee, chapter 10, C13th CE.

*highest God'*), who we have previously mentioned in connection to Kether. The soul is also likened to a lamp in the *Old Testament*, containing the divine light of the exiled Shekinah, thus in *Proverbs* we see, *"The human spirit is the lamp of the Lord."*[241]

The Gnostic Sophia was also associated with light, thus we see her described as *"the daughter of light"*.[242] The Gnostic Barbelo, another form of Sophia as a wisdom goddess, is described in *The Apocryphon of John*, as *"She is the forethought of the All - her light shines like his light"*.[243] *The Apocryphon of John* also states that *"Barbelo conceived and bore a spark of light"*.[244]

A powerful use of light is seen in *On the Origin of the World*, when Sophia sent archangels from her light, demonstrating her power as mother of angels:

> *"Then when Faith-Wisdom saw the war, she sent to Sabaoth from her light seven archangels."*[245]

The Manichean religion described the soul in terms of light as, *"the refined soul which they say is the daughter of light"*,[246] and also referred to Sophia as *"the Virgin of Light, the chief of all excellencies."*[247]

Another consideration of light is that of its role as a garment. Various references indicate raiment of light, and this is also implied in *Genesis* for Adam and Eve before they ate of the fruit of the Tree of Knowledge of Good and Evil, *"and they were both clothed in light, and saw not each*

---

241 Proverbs 20:27, C3rd BCE.
242 The Acts of Thomas, 50, C2nd CE, trans. M.R. James.
243 The Apocryphon of John, C2nd CE, trans. F Wisse.
244 Apocryphon of John, trans. Davies, C2nd CE.
245 On the Origin of the World, 104:17-19, C4th CE, trans F. Fallon.
246 St Ephrem I.71, C4th CE.
247 Turfan fragment M172, C8th-C10th CE.

*other's nakedness.*"[248] At a tangent from this, Scholem (1962:164) quotes a reference where *"In Manichean usage, too, the five limbs of the king of the paradise of light are called his five shekinoth."*[249]

The first light is the *Ain Soph Aur*, or Limitless Light, which predates physical manifestation. A Kabbalistic teaching is that the light (*Aur*, AVR) from the Ain Soph Aur was originally aether or spirit (*Auir*, AUIR). When the Ain Soph (limitlessness) became Ain Soph Aur, the spirit gave up its point (Yod, I), which was expressed in the first point of Kether, also known as the beginning of Tetragrammaton, the divine name of creation. Thus spirit (AVIR) became light (AVR) which could manifest (I).

The first Breath or emanation from Kether is known as Direct Light (*Aur Yashar*), which symbolises the principle of causality. Following from this is the Second Breath or Reflected Light (*Aur Chozer*) associated with Malkuth, and represents the effect of the cause. That light and breath are connected in Qabalah further reinforces the emphasis on the Shekinah, who embodies both these concepts.

Within the universe of the ten Sephiroth there is the Inner Light (*Aur Penimi*), or Inner Glory (*Kavod Penimi*) which illuminates the universe (note the Shekinah again as Kavod). Outside of this is the Light of the Quarry of Souls, and beyond that the Light of the Quarry of Angels. Beyond this is the Darkening Light, or Light of the Quarry of Husks (Qliphoth). Beyond the Darkening Light is the physical matter of the universe.

The Inner Light is the light of the divine, the Cosmic Shekinah permeating all of life. This is then expressed through the primal Adam Kadmon, through whom the *Shevirah*, or *"Breaking of the Vessels"*, occurred. This action was the inability of the lower Sephiroth of the first Tree of Life to contain the divine light expressed through Adam Kadmon, resulting in them shattering. The shards of

---

248 The Book of the Bee, chapter 14, C13th CE.
249 Origins of the Kabbalah, Scholem, 1962:164.

divine light which spread through the universe became clothed in matter and formed the human race.

These divine soul shards form the Light of the Quarry of Souls, the divine light which has literally been hewn from the primal Sephiroth, hence the use of the term *'quarry'*. These divine shards represent the highest aspect of the human soul, the Neshamah, or inner Shekinah.

The Light of the Quarry of Angels represents the role of the angels as messengers, enabling communication from the divine Inner Light of the Neshamah or Inner Shekinah to the Heavenly Shekinah who was the source of the light, acting as a connecting force.

The Light of the Quarry of Souls also acts as a barrier between the higher soul of the Neshamah and the unbalanced forces of the Qliphoth in the Light of the Quarry of Husks. This is why unbalanced forces act on the lower self (the *Nephesh*), the so-called *'base'* desires. There are also names given to types of light associated with specific Sephiroth on the Tree of Life. These are:

# Bahir

The word Bahir means *'brilliant'*, and is to be found in *Job* where it says "*Now, no one can look on the light when it is bright [brilliant] in the skies, when the wind has passed and cleared them. Out of the north comes golden splendour; around God is awesome majesty.*"[250] The reference to majesty and not seeing the light which is brilliant hint at Kether, suggests a light which is beyond human understanding. Also one of the most important Kabbalistic texts is the *Bahir*, which is one of the works which emphasises the Shekinah the most.

Although some Kabbalists associated Bahir light with Netzach, moving Nogah light to Geburah, this ignores the

---

250 Job 37:21-2, C3rd BCE.

concept that *"Bahir light is the shining glass, which has the power to reflect."*[251] The lights below are ultimately reflections, and that this light has the power to reflect indicates its generative nature (i.e. Kether).

# Kavod

Kavod means *'(divine) glory'*, and is used to describe the primeval light equated with both the Shekinah and her manifestation as the Ruach HaQadosh (*'Holy Spirit'*). The term can be applied both to invisible light and also its manifestation as the divine glory through the nine Sephiroth below Kether. This is best illustrated by a quote from Eleazer of Worms: *"The Kavod has nine colours: each twig of the nut-tree has nine leaves."*[252]

Scholem (1962:166), describing the Shekinah, emphasises the equation of Kavod to Shekinah, saying, *"it is called Kavod in the Bible, and Shekinah in the Rabbinic tradition."*[253] Wolfson (1994:43) expresses this more clearly, observing that:

> *"The rabbinic characterization of the divine presence (Shekinah) as light is based, of course, on similar descriptions of the glory (kavod) in biblical and apocalyptic sources."*[254]

---

251 Sepher Shekel haKodesh (The Book of the Holy Coin), Rabbi Moses de Leon, C13th CE.
252 Hokmath ha-Egoz, C13th CE.
253 Origins of the Kabbalah, Scholem, 1962:166.
254 Through a Speculum That Shines: Vision and Imagination in Medieval Jewish Mysticism, Wolfson, 1994:43.

# Tov

Tov means *'good'* and is the name for light associated with Chesed, the Sephira of Love. It is also associated with the Middle Pillar, another Shekinah symbol, as in *"God saw that the light was good (Ki Tov)"*,[255] showing how the light emanated above, below and in all directions.

# Nogah

Nogah (*'glow'*) is usually used to describe twilight, when the light of day (male) shines into the darkness of night (female). Hence it is used as a term for sexual union, which fits with its Venusian associations as the name of the Heaven of Netzach. The *'glow'* said to surround partners after making love is also an appropriate analogy to the light of Nogah.

Another important use of the word Nogah is in the Merkavah teachings, for the chariot described in *Ezekiel* 1:4 is said made of Nogah. This correlation is significant for its numerical symbolism, for Nogah is associated with seven (the number attributed to Venus in Qabalah) and the chariot rider travels through seven palaces.

# Zohar

Zohar means *'radiance'* or *'brightness'*, and it is associated with creative utterances through the extension of the initial point (such as the prophetic power of the Shekinah), thus it is said *"the Zohar which includes all*

---

255 Genesis 1:4, C10th-C8th BCE.

*letters and colours"*.[256] The significance of the name being given to one of the key texts, the *Zohar*, is clearly seen.

In some instances Zohar is the light associated with Hod, the Sephira whose name means *Splendour*. Zohar light is also described as being so intense (*Zahir*) that it is like the light of the sun.

# Chaim

Chaim means *'life'*, and is the light associated with the Sephira of Yesod. Yesod is associated with the sexual act and also the incarnation of the soul, and is thus highly appropriate for this type of light. As the higher soul (*Neshamah*) is a fragment of the Shekinah, then so Chaim light is also associated with the expression of the Shekinah.

| Type of Light | Meaning | Sephira |
|---|---|---|
| Bahir | Brilliant | Kether |
| Kavod | Glory | Chokmah-Malkuth |
| Tov | Good | Chesed/Tiphereth |
| Nogah | Glow | Netzach |
| Zohar | Radiance | Hod |
| Chaim | Life | Yesod |

# Menorah

The Menorah, or seven-pronged candlestick, is one of the most ancient symbols of Judaism, whose construction is described in the *Book of Genesis 25:31-40*. Its seven prongs symbolise many things, some of which are very pertinent here. The obvious symbolism is of the seven days of the week, with the central seventh candle placing representing the Sabbath. As the Shekinah is the Bride of the Sabbath it is easy to see that this central position would also correspond to her.

---

256 Zohar 1.15b, C13th CE.

The *Zohar* also describes how the reference in *Song of Solomon 3:7, "Look, it is the litter of Solomon! Around it are sixty mighty men of the mighty men of Israel"* is to the dwelling of the Shekinah, and the sixty (threescore) men represent the sixty angels who guard the Shekinah in heaven. The sixty also represent the six columns (of ten each) which surround the central flame of the Shekinah.

From a Qabalistic perspective, the three knops where the branches rise out from the central stem can be seen as the supernal triad of the Sephiroth of Kether, Chokmah and Binah, with Binah being the top knop. The seven candle branches represent the seven lower Sephiroth from Chesed to Malkuth, with Malkuth being the central candle placement for the Earthly Shekinah. Then we can see that as described in the *Thirty-Two Paths of Wisdom*, the Malkuth candle is *"sitting on the Throne of Binah"* which is below it.[257]

The seven branches also represent the seven heavens or palaces traversed by the Merkavah mystic seeking to enter the throne room of God. The almond blossom symbolism in the Menorah also corresponds to the Middle Pillar of the Tree of Life, as we can see in references such as the rod of Aaron budding fresh almonds,[258] and the rod of almond seen by Jeremiah at God's behest.[259]

A final consideration on light and the Shekinah is seen in connection with Moses. The reference indicates that the horns Moses are sometimes portrayed with from the power of the Shekinah. The *Midrash Tanhuma* on *Exodus 34:29* asks:

> *"'Whence did Moses get his horns of glory?' and comments, 'There are some who say that at the time when the Holy One taught Moses Torah, Moses gained his horns of glory from the sparks*

---

257 The Thirty-Two Paths of Wisdom, C11th CE.
258 Numbers 17.8, C8th-C5th BCE.
259 Jeremiah 1:11, C7th BCE.

*which shot out from the mouth of the Shekinah.'"*

It is not surprising that the different types of light should be so closely associated with the Shekinah, as her nature incorporates the primordial light of creation. Of course this is not the only one of her functions, as we will demonstrate in the following chapter, *Mother of Angels*.

# Mother of Angels

> *"Behold, I have revealed to you the name of the Perfect One, the whole will of the Mother of the Holy Angels."*
> ~ The Sophia of Jesus Christ, C4th CE, trans. Parrott

Considering the Kabbalistic model of creation as the result of the union of God and the Shekinah, the title of the Mother of Angels becomes entirely appropriate. The angels are the divine messengers (from *angelos*, *'messenger'*, Greek), and an interesting reference in *The Thunder, Perfect Mind* emphasises the association between the Wisdom Goddess (as Sophia in this instance) and angels, when she says: *"of the angels, who have been sent at my word."*[260] Angels are also described in one of the Merkavah texts as, *"Messengers of the Power and Awakeners of the Shekinah"*[261]

The *Zohar* makes reference to the angels being born from the Shekinah, saying, *"Its sparks are sparks of fire. Who are the sparks? Those gems and pearls born from that fire."*[262] It is also worth noting that the Shekinah is

---

260 The Thunder, Perfect Mind, C3rd-C4th CE, Nag Hammadi Texts, trans. George W. MacRae.
261 Hekhalot Rabbati, VII.154, C3rd-C7th CE.
262 Zohar 2:114a, C13th CE.

described as a gem and a pearl in Kabbalistic texts, demonstrating the continuity of association here.

A range of texts mention the connection between the Shekinah and angels, such as the first-third century CE *Gedulath Mosheh* (*The Revelation of Moses*), which describes:

> *"50 myriads of angels stand before him; they are of fire and water, and their faces are directed towards the Shekinah above; and all sing hymns"*[263]

Enoch describes his own ascension to heaven in the *Book of 3 Enoch,* saying that:

> *"When the Holy One, blessed be He, took me away from the generation of the Flood, he lifted me on the wings of the wind of Shekinah to the highest heaven and brought me into the great palaces of the Arabot Raqia on high, where are the glorious Throne of Shekinah, the Merkavah."*[264]

The references to wings and wind are significant, as both also occur in other sources, illustrating that the Heavenly Shekinah can be described as being winged, like the angels, and also that she has a significant relationship with the wind. An example of this can be found in the story of how Abraham founded the Kaaba at Mecca, where she is described as guiding him in the form of a stormy cloud or a wind with a tongue (i.e. speaking).[265]

The *Book of 3 Enoch* is full of descriptions of the presence of the Cosmic Shekinah in heaven. The greatest emphasis is placed on the four camps of the Shekinah and

263 The Revelation of Moses, 9, C1st-C3rd CE, trans. M. Gaster.
264 3 Enoch 7:1, C2nd-C6th CE.
265 Journeys in Holy Lands: the Evolution of the Abraham-Ishamel Legends in Islamic Exegesis, Firestone, 1990:68-71.

her throne, which is next to that of God, as we would expect for King and Queen together. The four camps are described as being ruled over by Gabriel, Michael, Raphael and Uriel (the archangels attributed to the four elements of Water, Fire, Air and Earth respectively). The camps are cited in the thirteenth century *Treatise on the Left Emanation*, which commented on the absence of form in the non-material highest heavens:

> *"The four encampments of the Divine Presence are nothing but spiritual emanations, in the image neither of bodies nor of bodily form".[266]*

The positions of the archangels ruling the camps in *3 Enoch* match the description in other Merkavah texts, such as the *Maaseh Merkavah* (*'the work of the Chariot'*). This suggests that it is possible that the four camps, with the Shekinah in the middle, may be the origin of the Jewish *Kriat Shema al ha-Mitah*, a powerful apotropaic prayer for protection[267] during sleep:

> *"In the name of Adonai the God of Israel:*
> *May the angel Michael be at my right,*
> *And the angel Gabriel be at my left;*
> *And in front of me the angel Uriel;*
> *And behind me the angel Raphael;*
> *And above my head the Shekinah."*

A similar formula to this prayer can be found on one of the Aramaic Incantation Bowls dating to around the fifth-sixth century CE which may illustrate its use as a common magical formula. It reads:

> *"On her right hand is Harbi'el, on her left hand is Michael, in front of her is Susi'el, and above*

---

266 Treatise on the Left Emanation, Isaac Ben Jacob ha-Kohen, C13th CE.
267 This prayer was adapted by the Hermetic Order of the Golden Dawn into the Lesser Banishing Ritual of the Pentagram in the late 19th century.

*her is the Shekinah of God and behind her is the word of Qaddish'el"*[268]

This emphasises an important point, being that as the Shekinah is the mother of angels, the angels then are also obvious intermediaries for her. Certain archangels are particularly associated with the Shekinah, i.e. Gabriel, Michael, Raphael and Uriel (the elemental archangels who rule her camps), as well as Metatron, the voice of God. These four elemental archangels have a long association together as rulers of the four elements, as seen in the numerous references to them together in magical rites and spells going back many centuries.

Significantly these four archangels are the only four also found in Islam, albeit with slightly alternative names or Arabic variants of some of their names, viz Uriel (Azrael), Gabriel (Jibrail) and Raphael (Israfel). Only Michael and Gabriel are named in the Bible, though Raphael is in the apocryphal *Book of Tobit,* and he and Uriel both appear in the pseudoepigraphical *Book of Enoch.*

# Metatron

The archangel Metatron is particularly associated with the Shekinah, as the highest of the angels. Metatron was described as being the prophet Enoch transformed into a being of pure flame (the archangel Metatron), who acted as the voice of God. He was known as the Prince of the Divine Countenance (*Malach ha-Panim*) or Angel of the Divine Countenance (*Sar ha-Panim*). The *Book of 3 Enoch* emphasises this when it states:

> *"R. Ishmael said: The angel Metatron, Prince of the Divine Presence, the glory of highest heaven, said to me: When the Holy One, blessed be he,*

268 Magic Spells and Formulae: Aramaic Incantation of Late Antiquity, Naved & Shaked, 1993, Bowl 22:2-3.

*took me to serve the throne of glory, the wheels of the chariot and all needs of the Shekinah, at once my flesh turned to flame".[269]*

It has been suggested that the name Metatron is derived from the Greek *Meta-Thronos*, meaning *'He who serves behind the Throne'*, referring to his high position in the presence of God (and the Shekinah who is also associayed with the Throne of Glory).[270] Considering the frequent references to the Throne of Glory in connection with Metatron this seems very plausible.

Metatron is described in *3 Enoch* as having seventy names, and several lists give Yahoel or its contraction of Yoel as the first of these. This is very significant both in the number seventy, which occurs in connection to the seventy sons of the goddess Athirat (another name for Asherah) who equate to the later seventy guardian angels of the nations, and also for the name Yoel.

Yoel occurs in the fourth century *Apocalypse of Zostrianos* in the *Nag Hammadi* texts as the name of as a hermaphroditic angel, being both male and female, and particularly connected with glory, *"Yoel, she of the glories, the male and virginal, came before me."*[271] The reference to glory also hints at the connection to the Shekinah, who is also known as Kavod (*'glory'*).

# Cherubs

*"And the Cherubim are standing by the holy Chayoth, and their wings are raised up to their heads and Shekinah is resting upon them and the brilliance of the glory is upon their faces ...*

269 3 Enoch 15:1, C2nd-C6th CE.
270 'Metatron', Lieberman, in Apocalyptic and Merkavah Mysticism, pages 235-241.
271 The Apocalypse of Zostrianos, Nag Hammadi Texts, C4th CE.

*and the splendour of Shekinah on their face and*
*Shekinah is resting upon them"*[272]

The Cherubim (or *Kerubim*, meaning '*Strong Ones'*) are the order of angels that are specifically mentioned in the *Old Testament* in various roles, which are commonly connected to the Shekinah. They are described as having human bodies and hands, with bronze calf's hooves, and two pairs of wings, of which one pair faced upwards and one pair downwards. Each angel had four faces, of man, with a lion on its right, an ox on the left and an eagle (presumably behind) (*Ezekiel 1:5-12*).

It was the Cherubim who guarded the gates of Eden after the Fall, when God, *"drove out the man; and at the east of the garden of Eden he placed the cherubim, and a sword flaming and turning to guard the way to the tree of life."*[273] As the *'flaming sword'* is another name for the lightning flash or path of creation on the Qabalistic Tree of Life, we can see that the Cherubim are guarding the way to the Shekinah, who as we have already seen is the Tree of Life.

The Shekinah is described in several sources as dwelling either at the base of the Tree of Life (i.e. Malkuth) or by the gate, and indeed is often seen as being the whole garden. This could be seen as referring to a golden age which man needs to regain, as described in Kabbalistic phrases like *'ascending to the orchard'*.

There were two Cherubim on the top of the Ark of the Covenant, which both faced inwards towards the mercy seat, from where Yahweh (or rather the Shekinah) spoke (*Exodus 25:10-22*). When Israel was faithfully worshipping Yahweh the Cherubs would embrace, symbolising the sacred marriage of Yahweh and the Shekinah, and of Israel's covenant to Yahweh.

---

272 3 Enoch 22:13, C2nd-C6th CE.
273 Genesis 3:24, C10th-C8th BCE.

Although angels are rarely named in the Bible (the exceptions being Michael and Gabriel), they do occur frequently as unnamed messengers of Yahweh. The importance of angels varies in different branches of Christian worship, but in Kabbalah and Merkavah mysticism they are a significant and regular force. As these are two primary areas of Shekinah source material, it is unsurprising to see such a close connection between angels and the Shekinah.

# The Breath of Life

> *"Ten Sefirot of Nothingness: One is the Breath of the Living God, Blessed and benedicted is the name of the Life of the Worlds, The voice of breath and speech And this is the Holy Breath [Ruach HaQadosh]."*
> ~ *Sepher Yetzirah 1:9, C2nd CE*

This verse from the second century CE *Sepher Yetzirah* is possibly the first specifically Kabbalistic reference hinting at the presence of the Shekinah (as Ruach HaQadosh) in the creation process. The Shekinah is associated with the breath, one of the most basic and fundamental manifestations of human existence and spirituality, and through this her connection with the soul is also made clear. The *Zohar* emphasises this connection between the Shekinah and breath, saying:

> *"'And the Lord God formed the man out of dust from the earth and breathed into his nostrils or soul the breath of life,' the divine Shekinah."*[274]

Looking at other cultures we find this association between breath and soul repeated. In Hinduism the *Atman* is the soul, and is derived from the Indo-European root

---

274 Zohar I.27a, C13th CE.

word for breath, *ēt-men*. In ancient Greece we see parallels of this association between breath and the soul with the Greek words *Thymos*, meaning 'breath', 'life', 'soul', 'courage', 'will'; and *Pneuma*, meaning 'breath', 'mind', or 'spirit'.

This further emphasises the interesting parallels with the philosophies of ancient Greece, which would influence Kabbalah through Neo-Platonism in the thirteenth-fifteenth century in Italy when both systems were blended with Hermeticism in the melting pot of Renaissance Italy.

One of the concepts expressed by Plato in his classic work *Phaedo*, derived from the teachings of the Greek philosopher Pythagoras (570-495 BCE) and his followers, was that the earth breathed through its subterranean tunnels, and volcanic eruptions were exhalations.

This idea of the earth as a being was emphasised again in the late twentieth century by the scientist James Lovelock with his Gaia Hypothesis, as previously mentioned. What is significant is that the importance of breathing was being emphasised on a cosmic or macrocosmic level.

The roots of the connection between the Shekinah and breath may come from the influence of the Egyptian goddess of truth, Ma'at, who was known as the breath of life for the sun god Ra. Interestingly the heart is particularly connected with Ma'at as well, being the part of the soul called the *ab* by the ancient Egyptians which was weighed against Ma'at's feather of truth on her scales to determine if the individual had led a virtuous life and was worthy of the company of the gods.

The verse in the *Sepher Yetzirah* describing the Hebrew letters which states *"He engraved them with voice, He carved them with breath, He set them in the mouth,"*[275] suggests that working with the breath may have been an important part of early Kabbalistic practice. However as for

---

275 Sepher Yetzirah 2:3, C2nd CE.

centuries Kabbalah was largely oral teaching, if this was the case such practices have largely been lost.

# Uniting the Soul

The Kabbalah describes the soul as having three main parts, the Neshamah, Ruach and Nephesh. The Neshamah has two further divisions, giving five parts in total. This is why the Hebrew letter Heh, with a numerical value of five, is often seen as being a symbol of the soul. Heh is also symbolic of the Shekinah in the divine name Tetragrammaton, a fact which is no coincidence.

So from the perspective of the Shekinah, the human soul is divided into the three major components of the *Neshamah* (higher soul) which is equated to the Earthly Shekinah as a spark of her fire, *Ruach* (middle soul) which may be equated to the Earthly Shekinah as the breath of life, and *Nephesh* (lower soul). These different parts of the soul are considered to each exist in a different world, demonstrating the interconnectedness of man, the universe and the Tree of Life as all being manifestations of the same creative divine impulse. The *Zohar*, on the subject of unification, states:

> *"Observe, when there is a just man in the world, or one whose higher and lower self have become harmonized and unified, the divine spirit or Shekinah is ever with him and abides in him, causing a feeling of affectionate attachment towards the Holy One to arise similar to that between the male and female."*[276]

Echoing the attribution of the Shekinah to the higher soul, some of the Gnostics also viewed the soul as feminine,

---

276 Zohar 1:66b, C13th CE.

as seen by the opening of *The Exegesis on the Soul* (one of the *Nag Hammadi* texts):

> *"Wise men of old gave the soul a feminine name. Indeed she is female in her nature as well. She even has her womb."*[277]

The Heavenly Shekinah is the cosmic soul of all, and this is made clear in the *Zohar*, which declares:

> *"When the moon - mystery of supernal nephesh - descends, illumined from all sides, She illumines all chariots and camps, forming them into one complete body shining with radiance, in supernal splendour. Similarly, this lower nephesh descends, illumined from all sides - from radiance of neshamah and radiance of ruach - and descending, she illumines all those chariots and camps."*[278]

The overwhelming aim to become righteous (*Tzaddiq*) and holy, and strive towards the return of the Shekinah from exile (i.e. to unite the soul) is the central theme in the writings of Rabbi Moses Chayim Luzatto in the eighteenth century. Luzatto was a contemporary of several significant figures, including the Baal Shem (founder of Hasidism), and Moses Mendelsohn (founder of Reform Judaism). He wrote:

> *"The pious scholars who are holy in their entire behaviour are actually like a sanctuary or an altar, because the Shekinah abides with them as it did in the sanctuary."*[279]

The higher parts of the *Neshamah*, namely the *Chayah* and the *Yechidah*, are known as *envelopments* (*makifim*), that is to say they are not perceived as being internalised

---

277 The Exegesis on the Soul, C4th CE, trans. W.C. Robinson Jr.
278 Zohar 2:242b, C13th CE.
279 Mesillat Yesharim, Luzatto, C18th CE.

within the human body. These more subtle components of the soul are believed to be present in the human aura, literally enveloping the body.

It is believed that these higher more subtle components of the soul can only be accessed through achieving an internal balance. This comes through inner harmony – first of the triad of the unconscious mind (Yesod), the intellect (Hod) and the emotions (Netzach). Next comes the harmony of will (Tiphereth), the passion and energy (Geburah), and love and righteousness (Chesed). When these six Sephiroth, known as the Sephiroth of Construction, have all been refined, the gateway of knowledge (Daath) is opened, permitting access to the higher divine self of the *Neshamah*/Shekinah (Binah), the *Chayah* (Chokmah) and the *Yechidah* (Kether).

In an important discussion of the generation of souls, the *Zohar* makes the hermaphroditic nature of the soul clear, saying,

> *"When souls issue, they issue male and female as one. Subsequently, as they descend they separate, one to this side, one to that side ... Happy is the human who acts virtuously, walking the way of truth, for soul is joined to soul as they were originally!"*[280]

Developing the idea of the hermaphroditic nature of the soul, the Hebrew words for man and woman both contain within them the mystery of the divine fire. The word for woman is *ishah* (Aleph Shin Heh) and the word for man is *isyh* (Aleph Yod Shin). If we remove the Heh from *ishah* and the Yod from *isyh* then both words become *esh* (Aleph Shin) meaning *'fire'*. So we can see that both women and men contain the same fire within them (the Shekinah), but the difference is in the manner of its manifestation and expression.

---

280 Zohar 1:85b, C13th CE.

This idea of the divine feminine soul fire is also seen in the *Chaldean Oracles of Zoroaster*, which recorded that, *"The Soul, being a brilliant Fire, by the power of the Father remaineth immortal, and is Mistress of Life, and filleth up the many recesses of the bosom of the World."*[281]

The Yod from *isyh* (man) represents the masculine principle as the Father in Tetragrammaton, and in appearance it represents the phallus and the sperm. The Heh from *ishah* (woman) represents the feminine principle as the Mother (and daughter) in Tetragrammaton, and in appearance it represents the legs. The union of Yod and Heh gives the Divine Name Yah, attributed to Wisdom (the Sephira of Chokmah). Yah is the first part of Tetragrammaton (Yah-Veh) and is known as the Inner Chamber, referring to sexual union.

# The Lower Soul

The *Nephesh* ('*Resting Soul*') is the lowest part of the soul, representing the animal nature of mankind, the cravings and instincts. The *Nephesh* is of the world of Yetzirah, corresponding to the Astral Triad, the Sephiroth of Netzach, Hod and Yesod. However it is also connected to the world of Assiah, corresponding to Malkuth, as it is the raw energy of life which makes the body (*Guph*) function. When a person dies the Nephesh does not ascend to higher realms, but remains in the physical world even after the death of the body and transmigration of the higher soul.

The earthly presence of the *Nephesh*, as present in the blood during life, and passing into the earth on death was hinted at in the earliest Biblical texts. Thus in *Genesis 4:10*, when Cain has slain Abel his deed is revealed by Abel's *Nephesh*, as shown when *"God said: 'What have you done? The voice of your brother's blood is screaming to Me from the ground."*

---

281 Chaldean Oracles of Zoroaster, 20, C2nd CE.

This theme of the *Nephesh* resting in the earth after death is also seen in *1 Samuel 28*. Saul went to the witch and persuaded her to perform an act of necromancy and raise the shade of Samuel (i.e. his *Nephesh*). When she performs her ritual the witch sees the shade *"coming up out of the ground."*[282] In these two passages the Bible effectively provides an explanation of the practice of necromancy within the Jewish cosmology.

The *Book of Deuteronomy* also refers to the presence of the Nephesh in the blood, in the stricture which explains the importance of removing the blood from kosher meat in Judaism:

> *"Be extremely careful not to eat the blood: since the blood is associated with the spiritual nature (life-force), and when you eat flesh, you shall not ingest the spiritual nature along with it. Since you must not eat the blood, you can pour it on the ground like water."*[283]

# The Middle Soul

The *Ruach* (*'wind'* or *'spirit'*) is the middle soul or spirit, sometimes known as the Intellectual Spirit, which is associated with the Shekinah as the breath of life by the *Zohar*.[284] The *Ruach* is of the world of Briah, corresponding to the Ethical Triad, the Sephiroth of Tiphereth, Geburah and Chesed.

As an expression of the Earthly Shekinah within the individual, the *Ruach* is the seat of moral qualities divided into five sub-parts, corresponding to the faculties of Memory, Will, Imagination, Desire and Reason. Note the five sub-parts corresponding to the number five as a symbol of the Shekinah and the five parts of the soul.

---

282 1 Samuel 28:13, C10th-C8th CE.
283 Deuteronomy 12:23-24, C7th BCE.
284 Zohar I.27a, C13th CE.

In *The Apocryphon of John*, Pronoia (Divine Providence manifesting as Barbelo) performs what could be seen as an initiation on the soul, when she enters into the body (described as a prison) and brought her light to bear on the soul:

> *"And I raised him up, and sealed him in the light of the water with five seals, in order that death might not have power over him from this time on."*[285]

There may also be a parallel here between these five faculties and the five limbs or members referred to in the *Acts of Thomas* when it says, *"Come, elder of the five members, mind, thought, reflection, consideration, reason."*[286]

The *Ruach* is associated with inspiration and prophecy, which fits with its meaning of either *'wind'* or *'spirit'*. We see clear parallels to the *Ruach* in the Greek words *Thymos*, (*'breath'*, *'life'*, or *'soul'*) and *Pneuma* (*'breath'*, *'mind'*, or *'spirit'*).

# The Higher Soul

The *Neshamah* is the upper soul, breath or pneuma, and is also referred to as the Shekinah. It is first referred to in *Genesis 2:7* - *"Then the Lord God formed man of the dust of the ground, and breathed into his nostrils the breath of life; and man became a living soul [Neshamah]."*

The *Neshamah* is always depicted as being female, and all women are said to be in the shelter of the Shekinah, resulting in the belief that it is easier for a woman to reach the *Neshamah* than a man. The higher aspects of the *Neshamah* remain unknown and unknowable to a person

---

285 The Apocryphon of John, C2nd CE, trans. F. Wisse.
286 The Acts of Thomas, 27, C2nd CE, trans. M.R. James.

until they have become aware of their *Neshamah*. It is also said that all people see the *Neshamah* at the moment of death.

In Christianity the Shekinah as the soul did not simply disappear. As Francis Peters observed,

> *"What was called by the Jews the Shekinah, the Divine Presence, became for Eastern Christians the Divine Light, which 'illuminates the soul from within'."*[287]

The principle is that for a person to progress spiritually they must have refined their *Nephesh* and *Ruach* and harmonised these with their *Neshamah*. This is why the *Zohar* says of the parts of the soul that, *"all three are one, comprising a unity, embraced in a mystical bond."*

In Jewish folklore the *Neshamah* is said to be seen at the moment of death, so even if a person has led a completely unspiritual life, they will catch a glimpse of the Shekinah at their death. This belief is referred to in the Adeptus Major initiation ritual of the Fellowship of the Rosy Cross, where the candidate is told, *"Shekinah, Mother in transcendence, grant that in his death he may behold Thy Holy Face, that he may know the life which is Thou."*[288]

The idea of initiates gaining visions of the Shekinah may stem from the Hebrew concept of the *Lamed-Vavniks* (*'The Thirty-Six'*). These are said to be the minimum number of righteous people required in each generation to sustain the world.[289] It seems likely that the number of thirty-six is derived from the number of Decans (arcs of 10°) in the Zodiac, which were personified in the ancient world by

---

287 Judaism, Christianity, and Islam: the classical texts and their interpretation, Peters, 1990, p235.
288 Adeptus Major Ritual, Fellowship of the Rosy Cross, 1916.
289 The Encyclopedia of Jewish Myth, Magic and Mysticism, Dennis, 2007:149.

demons[290] and holy men.[291] Most of the thirty-six righteous people are said to be unknown in their lifetimes, working good anonymously, and being rewarded with direct experience of the Shekinah as their reward.

# The Living Essence

The Chayah (or Chiyah or Chiah, meaning *"life force"* or *"living essence"*) is described as a higher aspect of the Neshamah that is the vitality, the creative impulse. This is often equated to the will or intent.

# The Unique Essence

The Yechidah (*"unique essence"* or *"unity"*) is considered the highest aspect of the Neshamah, and can be seen as corresponding to the divine and immortal spark of the soul that is part of the eternal Shekinah. It is the most ephemeral and transcendental part of the soul, where the highest essence of man becomes the divine.

| Part of Soul | World | Sephiroth | Impulse |
|---|---|---|---|
| Yechidah | Atziluth | Kether | Divinity |
| Chayah | Atziluth | Chokmah | Intent |
| Neshamah | Atziluth | Binah | Thought |
| Ruach | Briah | Chesed Geburah Tiphereth | Speech |
| Nephesh | Yetzirah | Netzach Hod Yesod | Action |
| Guph (body) | Assiah | Malkuth | Manifestation |

290 The Testament of Solomon, C2nd CE.
291 Animal-Headed Gods, Evangelists, Saints and Righteous Men, Ameisenowa, 1949:33.

# The Platonic Model

The Greek philosopher Plato drew on the philosophies of his teacher Socrates (469-399 BCE) to formulate his views on the nature of the soul. Plato's model of the soul was a three part one, which he considered eternal and intangible, and which reincarnated through subsequent physical bodies. Plato named the three parts as the *logos* or *nous*, the *thymos* and the *eros* or *epithumia*.

Plato described the highest part of the soul as the *logos* (or nous, *'intellect'*), which was the mind and reason, and was the divine part of the soul. The middle part of the soul he called the *thymos* (*'breath'* or *'soul'*), the emotional part which could lift a person to courage or drag them into pride depending on their motives. The lowest part of the soul he called the *eros*, which he viewed as passion in this context rather than its other meaning as physical love, or the *epithumia* (*'appetite'*); it represented the desires and passions that motivate the self, and need to be controlled to prevent the descent into hedonism.

These three parts correspond closely in many ways to the Neshamah, the Ruach and the Nephesh, leading to the inevitable conclusion that Plato's teachings influenced those in the Kabbalah. When we remember that the development of the Kabbalah in the early Middle Ages and Renaissance coincided with the retranslation of the Neo-Platonic texts of such notable Greek philosophers as Plotinus (204-270 CE) and Proclus (412-485 CE), this becomes even more apparent.

# The Egyptian Model

The Egyptians believed in the plurality of the soul, i.e. that it was comprised of many parts, which had different roles and which did not all remain united together after death. This fragmentation of the parts of the soul is

178

something which is subsequently found in both the Greek and Hebrew models of the parts of the soul.

As with a number of other philosophical and theological concepts, it is likely that both the ancient Greeks and the Hebrews integrated ideas learned from the Egyptians into their practices. Alternatively the idea may have been transmitted from the Egyptians to the Greeks and on to the Hebrews.

| Part of the Soul | Function |
|---|---|
| Ab | The heart, centre of moral awareness and good and evil. The Ab lived with the gods if it passed judgement, balancing Ma'at's feather of Truth. |
| Akhu | Meaning *'effective one'*, the radiant immortal part of the person, created by the uniting of Ba and Ka and residing in the Sahu. |
| Ba | Can be translated as *'impression'*, and was depicted as a human-headed bird, this part of the soul represented the personality of the person. |
| Ka | The life-force. |
| Khabait | The shadow, that could partake of funerary offerings for sustenance, and leave the tomb. |
| Ren | The true name of a person, describing their essence. |
| Sahu | The vessel of the spiritual body. |
| Sekhem | The ethereal personification of the life force of the person. |

Comparatively we can suggest that the Ka would equate to the Nephesh, and the Ba with the Ruach. The Ab would equate to the Neshamah, the Sekhem to the Chayah, and the Ren to the Yechidah. Obviously this is not an exact match as we are comparing two different theologies, but the parallels are clear. Indeed if we compare across to the Greek Platonic model as well, we see the following equation of systems:

179

| Part of the Soul | Qabalah | Platonic | Egyptian |
|---|---|---|---|
| Mind, divine spark | Neshamah | Nous/Logos | Ab |
| Personality, emotions | Ruach | Thymos | Ba |
| Vitality, instinct | Nephesh | Eros/Epithumia | Ka |

# Gilgul

The idea of reincarnation, or transmigration of souls, known as *gilgul* (meaning *'revolving'* or *'swirling'*) was one that became integrated into Qabalistic belief, being first published in the *Bahir* in the late thirteenth century CE. Again there may have been a Neo-Platonic influence here as the doctrine of transmigration of souls was found in a number of Neo-Platonic writings.

On death the parts of the soul all go to their appointed places. The *Nephesh* sinks into the earth, to go to *Gehinnom* (hell) if the person has been bad, the *Ruach* stays with the body, and the *Neshamah* ascends to the Throne of God, where the Shekinah sustains it until it is ready to descend back into physical form.

The *Zohar* describes how the *Neshamah* is clothed in a bodily garment to exist in the world, and in a garment of light to exist in heaven, mirroring the Earthly Shekinah and the Heavenly Shekinah.[292]

This doctrine is hinted at by the name of the heaven of the highest Sephira, Kether, i.e. *Rashith ha-Gilgalim* (the first swirlings), coming from the same root as the word *gilgul.* The soul aspires to its highest aspect, the *Yechidah,* seeking to elevate the lower aspects so they may be united with the highest and then re-merge with the ultimate divine.

---

292 Zohar 1.65b-66a, C13th CE.

There are a number of variants of this belief, such as where the souls go depending on conduct. A soul that has fulfilled its spiritual destiny does not need to continue reincarnating, and is said to be stored in holiness by God until the end of time, when it is rejoined with its body, its *Ruach* and its *Nephesh*.

God will then cause dew (which is the divine light) to exude from His head that will flow through the Sephiroth until it reaches the earth. The dew is said to be that which would have caused Adam and Eve to have become immortal, and will enable the resurrected soul to be remerged with the primal Adam or the Heavenly Shekinah. In this way every person is part of the process of restoration (*tikkun*).

A soul that has knowingly perpetrated evil will return to a lesser form, such as an animal, plant or even stone. This doctrine is analogous to the Hindu concept of karmic reincarnation, and is thought to have its roots in Platonic and Neo-Platonic philosophies. This is made even clearer in the *Zohar*, which raises the issue of reincarnation in an interesting manner, with discussion of the final judgement. It says:

> "Said Rabbi Hizkiah: 'If it be so that all the dead bodies will rise up from the dust, what will happen to a number of bodies which shared in succession the same soul?' Rabbi Jose answered: ' Those bodies which were unworthy and did not achieve their purpose will be regarded as though they had not been: as they were a withered tree in this world, so will they be regarded at the time of the resurrection. Only the last that had been firmly planted and took root and prospered will come to life, as it says, 'For he shall be as a tree planted by the waters ... but its foliage shall be luxuriant (Jer 17:8).'"[293]

---

293 Zohar 1.131a, C13th CE.

A later version of this doctrine changed the concept of rebirth until perfection is reached with a cycle of only four incarnations. If by the end of the fourth life the soul had not reached a basic level of development it would roam the earth as a spirit (called a *dybbuk*) that sought to possess other people to control their bodies and be returned to the flesh. If the soul did reach a level of attainment it would find sanctuary until the day of restitution.

The *Bahir* also refers to reincarnation, making veiled and symbolic comments such as,

> *"It is I who have planted this 'tree' that the whole world may delight in it ... for on it depends the All and from it emanates the All; all things need it and look upon it and yearn for it, and it is from it that all souls fly forth."*

More clearly, the *Bahir* also describes transmigration of souls through the parable of the king's servants and their garments. The servants mistreat their fine garments so the king throws them out and cleans the garments and dresses other servants in them, giving them garments which have already been worn in the world.

Looking at other early influential cultures, we see that the ancient Egyptians did not subscribe to that idea, with a person living one life and then either joining the gods if they had led a good enough life or being annihilated if they had not.

The *Chaldean Oracles of Zoroaster* refers to reincarnation, saying, *"According to Zoroaster, in us the ethereal vestment of the Soul perpetually revolves [reincarnates]."*[294] In the *Chaldean Oracles*, there is a similar concept to the Shekinah of a goddess who is both the world soul, and also the source of souls, though there it is the Greek goddess Hekate. The *Chaldean Oracles* were written after many centuries of Hekate's worship, so it is

---

294 Chaldean Oracles of Zoroaster, 97, C2nd CE.

possible that these qualities may have been assimilated from the influence of other cultures and ideologies like the Jews and Gnosticism.

As with the Tree of Life and types of light, it is clear that the Shekinah is also intimately bound up with ideas of the soul in Kabbalah and Jewish mysticism. Like the Shekinah herself, the roots of these ideas can be seen in earlier cultures, as we have demonstrated by comparatively exploring the Platonic and Egyptian models of the soul.

The equation of the Shekinah to the Neshamah gives basis to the idea that every soul not only comes from the same original source, but also every soul is also connected. This relationship of the Shekinah and souls emphasises how often she is connected with mystical concepts.

# The Power of Prophecy

> *"Human souls are also bound to higher levels, and therefore, when a perfect individual becomes involved in meditation upon wisdom, it is possible for him to predict future events."*
> ~ Hai Gaon (939-1038 CE)

The word prophet is derived from the ancient Greek word *'prophetia'*, meaning *'the gift of interpreting the will of the gods'*. This emphasises the nature of a prophet, who was considered not simply a person who could see the future (such as a clairvoyant or seer), but rather a person who was divinely inspired and could relay the inspirations and messages they received.

In more recent decades it has also come to be applied to people who made predictions about the future, i.e. demonstrated precognition, such as the French doctor Nostradamus (1503-1566 CE) and the American psychic Edgar Cayce (1877-1945 CE).

The Hebrew word *Tanakh* (TNK), the name for the *Old Testament* is Notariqon (an acronym) for *Torah Neviim Ketuvim*, meaning *'Law, Prophets, Writings'*, indicating the three divisions of the holy books in order of decreasing divine revelation, and emphasising the importance of prophecy.

In Judaism prophecy was believed to have stopped after the destruction of the Temple in Jerusalem, as the Heavenly Shekinah withdrew and her holy spirit of inspiration was no longer available to prophets. In Islam too, prophecy was believed to have stopped with the death of the Prophet Mohammed in 632 CE.

Although the prophets of the *Old Testament* are popularly thought of as being men, there were also female prophetesses, with seven of the fifty-five mentioned in the *Old Testament* being women. The most famous of the prophetesses was Miriam, the sister of Aaron and Moses, who is referred to in *Exodus*.

The other very famous prophetess was Deborah, whose story is told in the eight century BCE *Book of Judges 5*, also known as *The Song of Deborah*. *The Song of Deborah* is often credited with earlier roots, possibly as early as the twelfth century BCE.

A curious dichotomy in this text is that Deborah is referred to as *Lapidot-woman*, which could be a (husband's) name or a noun, which would mean *'woman of torches'*. This connection with torches, and hence fire and light, is an interesting one which recalls the common association of torches with other goddesses, including Hekate. It is particularly relevant when the parallels between Deborah and the Semitic goddess Anat are seen. As Taylor (1982:92-108) points out, the *Song of Deborah* has a number of parallels with earlier Ugaritic literature which support the ideas that this piece is one of the earliest sections of the *Old Testament*, and that it preserves one of the Anat tales in a derivative form, describing the conquest of Canaan.[295]

Returning to the practice of prophecy, it should be noted that prophecy was not seen as a natal gift that a person was born with; rather it was the culmination of a

---

[295] The Song of Deborah and Two Canaanite Goddesses, Taylor, 1982:82-108.

holy life, resulting in the Shekinah descending on a person as the Ruach HaQadosh (Holy Spirit).

The Roman writer (Saint) Hippolytus (c.170-236 CE) wrote in his *Refutation of All Heresies* of how some women prophetesses claimed to be possessed by the *Paraclete* (the Greek term for *Ruach HaQadosh*, the Holy Spirit) and this detracted from the true Christianity.[296] It is interesting to note how his venom was reserved for women, which significantly differed from the reported teachings of the prophet Elijah, which declared:

> *"I call heaven and earth to witness that any person, Jew or Gentile, man or woman, freeman or slave, if his deeds are worthy, then Ruach HaQadosh will descend upon him."*[297]

The association of the Shekinah with the power of prophecy, or Ruach HaQadosh, is a well established one. Saadia Gaon (882-942 CE), the founder of Judeo-Arabic literature, made this significant connection in his writings. He stated:

> *"The luminous manifestation which must validate for the prophet the authenticity of the revelation he has received is a created light; it is called kavod in the Bible, and Shekinah in the Rabbinic tradition."*[298]

However many centuries earlier this association between the Wisdom Goddess and prophecy was already implied by the connection between the Canaanite goddess Asherah and divination. A fifteenth century BCE tablet found at Taanach in northern Palestine contains the line:

> *"Further, and if there is a wizard of Asherah, let him tell our fortunes, and let me hear quickly(?);*

---

296 Refutation of All Heresies 8.13, Hippolytus, C2nd CE.
297 Tana DeBei Eliahu 9, date unknown, recorded in C16th CE.
298 Sepher 'Emunoth we-De'oth, Saadia, C10th CE

*and the (oracular) sign and interpretation send to me."[299]*

The association between the Wisdom Goddess and prophecy was also made in the last of the great Jewish wisdom texts, the *Wisdom of Solomon* (first century BCE), which declared:

> *"She is but one, yet can do all things, herself unchanging, she makes all things new; age after age she enters into holy souls, and makes them friends of God and prophets."[300]*

The philosopher and poet Judah Halevi (1075-1141 CE) writing in Arabic described the connection between the Shekinah and the availability of the power of prophecy:

> *"Prophecy accompanied the community of the Second Temple forty years, on account of the elders who were assisted by the power of the Shekinah which was present in the First Temple. [Newly] acquired prophecy ceased with the departure of the Shekinah, and only came at extraordinary times or on account of [a] great force, such as that of Abraham, Moses, the expected Messiah, Elijah and their equals. For they in themselves were a dwelling place (mahall) of the Shekinah, and their very presence helped those present to acquire the degree of prophecy."[301]*

Continuing on this theme, the medieval Kabbalist Abraham Abulafia (1240-1291 CE) described the connection between the Shekinah and prophecy when he wrote:

---

299 Asherah in the Hebrew Bible and Northwest Semitic Literature, Day, 1986:386.
300 Wisdom of Solomon, 7:27, C1st BCE.
301 The Kuzari 3.65, 137, Judah Halevi, 1140 CE.

*"Yod bears witness to the Throne that is the height of Heh, up to the height of the Vav .... And the final Heh is Shekinah's seal, the inspiration offering prophecy and salvation to all souls by her Voice and lightness."*[302]

In his classic work *Gates of Light* on how to achieve states of Ruach HaQadosh, Rabbi Chaim Vital (1543-1620 CE) distinguished between what he considered to be the two types of prophecy, and also clarified the difference between prophecy and dreams.

*"The difference between prophecy and dream is that in the former the Nephesh remains in the Guph (body), whereas in the latter the Nephesh leaves the body."*[303]

Significantly Vital described how the prophecy of the prophets involved the withdrawal and collapse of the external senses due to the overpowering influence of the Shekinah's light (number 8 on the list of Maimonides categories). The second type of prophecy does not result in the senses withdrawing, but provides a pure image, as was the case for Moses (number 12 on the list of Maimonides categories).

Vital, like most medieval Kabbalists, would have drawn inspiration from the twelfth century Jewish philosopher Moses Maimonides (1135-1204 CE). In his epic three volume work outlining his philosophies, *The Guide for the Perplexed* (*Moreh Nevuchim*), Maimonides described the twelve stages of prophecy. Looking at his list it is interesting to note that many people will have experienced some or most of the first five categories of prophecy he gives.

---

302 Sepher Ha-Ot (The Book of the Letter), Abulafia, 1285-88 CE.
303 Shaarei Kedusha, Vital, C16th CE.

# Maimonides Prophecy Categories

| Category | Form | Notes |
|---|---|---|
| 1 | Inspired actions | |
| 2 | Inspired words | |
| 3 | Allegorical dream revelations | Symbolic images which may need deciphering |
| 4 | Dream revelations | Made by an unseen voice |
| 5 | Dream revelations | Made by a human speaker, audiovisual |
| 6 | Dream revelations | Made by an angel, audiovisual |
| 7 | Dream revelations | Made by divinity, audiovisual |
| 8 | Allegorical waking vision | Symbolic images which may need deciphering |
| 9 | Waking revelation | Made by an unseen voice |
| 10 | Waking revelation | Made by a human speaker, audiovisual |
| 11 | Waking revelation | Made by an angel, audiovisual |
| 12 | Waking revelation | Made by divine presence, refers to e.g. Moses and the Shekinah in burning bush |

The categories of Maimonides clearly disagreed with the Jewish and Islamic view that prophecy was no longer possible.

The *Torah* is full of references and hint regarding the power of prophecy (precognition), which give indicators on how to achieve this ability, or state, which is known as Ruach HaQadosh, the *'Spirit of Holiness'* or *'Holy Spirit'*. This is also another name for the Shekinah, who is thus the bestower of prophecy, the divine wisdom which is her domain.

This is referred to explicitly in *Psalm 51:12-13*, where it says:

*"Create in me a clean heart, O God, and put a new and right spirit within me. Do not cast me away from your presence, and do not take your holy spirit from me."*

One of the useful adjuncts to achieving a suitable state for prophecy was considered to be music. Music can strongly influence the emotions, and help create a serene state ideal for meditation. The use of instrumental music, without lyrics (there is no reference to singing) is thus a precursor that can be used to help achieve the state of Ruach HaQadosh. Rabbi Moses Maimonides explains this in his writings, saying:

*"A prophet cannot prophesy at will. He concentrates his mind, sitting in a good, joyous mood and meditating. One cannot attain prophecy when he is depressed and languid, but only when he is in a joyous state. When they were seeking prophecy, the prophets would therefore have people play music for them."*[304]

Significantly two of the Psalms begin by referring to music, indicating their use as an aid to prophecy. Thus we see reference to string music in *Psalms* 4 and 6. This is also indicated in several of the Biblical books where musical instruments are specifically connected with prophecy.[305] The most explicit reference to this is in *1 Samuel 10:5-6*, where it says:

*"You will meet a band of prophets coming down from the shrine with harp, tambourine, flute, and lyre playing in front of them; they will be in a prophetic frenzy. Then the spirit of the Lord*

---

304 Yad, Yesodey HaTorah 7:4, Rabbi Moses Maimonides C12th CE.

305 2 Kings 3:15 (C7th BCE), 1 Chronicles 25:1 (C3rd BCE), 1 Samuel 10:5-6 (C10th-C8th BCE).

*will possess you, and you will be in a prophetic frenzy along with them and be turned into a different person."*[306]

An interesting hint in this text is that the prophets were *'coming down'* from the shrine, i.e. it was in a high place. This reference then suggests that the prophets may have been of a deity associated with worship in high places, i.e. the goddess Asherah.

Another sound associated with prophecy is humming. The Hebrew Mother letter Mem is associated with humming,[307] as the water of Chokmah (Wisdom). This association is described in the *Book of Job*, though the word hum has also been translated as silence, with a graphic and lucid description of the experience of Ruach HaQadosh:

> *"Now a word came stealing to me,*
> *my ear received the whisper of it.*
> *Amid thoughts from visions of the night,*
> *when deep sleep falls on mortals,*
> *dread came upon me, and trembling,*
> *which made all my bones shake.*
> *A spirit glided past my face;*
> *the hair of my flesh bristled.*
> *It stood still,*
> *but I could not discern its appearance.*
> *A form was before my eyes;*
> *there was silence [a hum], then I heard a*
> *voice:"*[308]

The modern Kabbalist Aryeh Kaplan (1934-1983 CE) discussed the requirements for achieving prophecy,[309] stating that it is a step-by-step process requiring thorough mastery, using disciplines including meditation, reciting

---

306 1 Samuel 10:5-6, C10th-C8th BCE.
307 Sepher Yetzirah 2:1, C2nd CE.
308 Job 4:12-16, C3rd BCE.
309 See Meditation and the Bible, 1978:65-8.

Divine Names, and praising God with prayers containing the Divine names. He emphasised that attachment to God and continual purification are also required, with the achievement of Ruach HaQadosh not being an easy achievement, but rather a process that requires great devotion and dedication.

The descriptions in the *Torah* suggest that the type of meditation that was used was void meditation, i.e. the removal of all awareness of the body. This is indicated in the Psalms, *"Whom have I in heaven but you? And there is nothing on earth that I desire other than you. My flesh and my heart may fail, but God is the strength of my heart and my portion forever."*[310]

Timing was also considered important, with night and dusk being the best time to meditate. Thus we see, *"My eyes are awake before each watch of the night, that I may meditate on your promise."*,[311] and *"Arise, cry out in the night, at the beginning of the watches! Pour out your heart like water before the presence of the Lord!"*[312]

Perhaps the best description was given by Rabbi Jacob ben Asher (1270-1343 CE), who wrote:

> *"One must concentrate on the words that leave his lips, depicting the Divine Presence right in front of him, as it is written, 'I have placed God before me at all times' [Psalms 16:8]. He must arouse his concentration, removing all disturbing thoughts so that his mind and concentration in prayer remain pure."*[313]

The *Talmud* also describes the ten steps which lead to Ruach HaQadosh. These correspond to the Sephiroth of the Tree of Life. These steps are:

---

310 Psalm 73:25-26, C10th-C2nd BCE.
311 Psalm 119:148, C10th-C2nd BCE.
312 Lamentations 2:19, C6th BCE.
313 Tur, Orach Chain, 98, Rabbi Jacob ben Asher, C14th CE.

1. Study [Malkuth]
2. Carefulness [Yesod]
3. Diligence [Hod]
4. Cleanliness [Netzach]
5. Abstention [Tiphereth]
6. Purity [Geburah]
7. Piety [Chesed]
8. Humility [Binah]
9. Fear of Sin [Chokmah]
10. Holiness [Kether]

From all these writings it is clear that the view that prophecy stopped with the destruction of the Temple in Jerusalem was not one shared by many Kabbalists, who wrote of the methods used to achieve prophetic states, by developing their connection to the Shekinah, the source of prophecy.

In addition to the Kabbalists with the Shekinah, the Gnostics, too made reference to prophecy received from Sophia (or unnamed feminine wisdom) in their writings, as may be seen in the text of *Trimorphic Protennoia*:

> *"I am the Mother of the Voice, speaking in many ways, completing the All. It is in me that knowledge dwells, the knowledge of <things> everlasting. It is I who speak within every creature, and I was known by the All. It is I who lift up the Speech of the Voice to the ears of those who have known me, that is, the Sons of the Light."[314]*

From her later attribution to *Old Testament* references, the Shekinah has a fundamental connection with prophecy, being viewed as the divine power which provides the inspiration which prophets draw from.

---

314 Trimorphic Protennoia, C4th CE, trans. J.D. Turner.

This perspective challenges notions as to when prophecy ceased to become available, with many Kabbalistic writings crediting the influence of the Shekinah with the continuation of prophecy beyond the destruction of the temple in Jerusalem. It also challenges gender stereotypes of prophecy, making it clear that the Shekinah's inspiration may be drawn on by any suitably purified and spiritually prepared person.

# Part 5

# Fruits of the Tree

# The Renaissance & Beyond

> *"I, tranced, beheld an awful glory. Sphere in sphere it burned: the one Shekinah!"*
> *~ Mardi, Melville, 1849*

We have shown how the Shekinah rose to new prominence in medieval Kabbalah, which emphasised her roles and power in a dramatic way. One of the biggest influences of the Kabbalah during the medieval and Renaissance period was on the grimoires, books which gave detailed techniques for conjuring angels and/or demons, and for making talismans to attract all sorts of wonders and wealth.

So the obvious question is did the Shekinah also made the transition into the grimoires, which had a significant influence on the development of modern magic? The answer is yes, we can find evidence of the Shekinah in the grimoires, if we look carefully.

We have already described how the Greek term *Paraclete* for the Holy Spirit was applied to prophetesses who were inspired by the divine wisdom, i.e. the

Shekinah.[315] Paraclete (as Paracletus) was one of the divine words, like Yahveh, Adonai and Sabaoth (Tzabaoth) which would be used to command spiritual beings in the *Heptameron* (*'Seven Days'*), written by the Italian physician Peter de Abano (1250-1317 CE) and published posthumously in 1496 CE.

The *Heptameron* was one of the most significant and influential of the grimoires, and was essentially a manual of planetary angel magic, which included the four archangels who ruled over the camps of the Shekinah, i.e. Gabriel, Michael, Raphael and Uriel.

Subsequent texts would reproduced this use of the term Paracletus, and it appears in the seventeenth century grimoire called the *Goetia* (*'howling'*), as a commanding name for demons, and likewise in *The Discoverie of Witchcraft* (1584) by the English author Reginald Scot (1538-1599 CE).

Other expressions in the same conjurations also imply the Shekinah through descriptions of the wisdom of God, the angels, throne and fire, and indicate it is not an isolated and misplaced incident:

> *"And by O Theos Iscyros Athanatos Paracletos ... And by the four beasts that stood before the throne having eyes before and behind, and by the fire round about the throne, And by the holy Angels of heaven, And by the mighty wisdom of God,"*[316]

The Elizabethan astrologer, mathematician and magus Dr John Dee (1527-1608 CE) performed years of work with his skryer Edward Kelley trying to gain divine wisdom with the assistance of the angels. One of the results of their work was a language called Enochian, which was said to be

---

315 Refutation of All Heresies, Hippolytus, 8.13, C2nd CE.
316 The Second Conjuration, The Goetia of Dr Rudd, Skinner & Rankine, 2007:177.

spoken by the angels. A series of calls in Enochian were transmitted to Dee via Kelley, along with English translations of the otherwise unintelligible words. Amongst these the Second Call is full of Shekinah symbolism, and it is also interesting to note the occurrence of the term 'seething', remembering that the name Barbelo (for the Gnostic wisdom goddess) may come from a root meaning 'to seethe':

> "Can the wings of the winds understand your voices of wonder, o you the second of the First? Whom the burning flames have framed within the depths of my jaws; Whom I have prepared as cups for a wedding, or as the flowers in their beauty for the chamber of righteousness. Stronger are your feet than the barren stone, and mightier are your voices than the manifold winds; for you are become a building such as is not, but in the mind of the All-Powerful. Arise, says the First; move, therefore, unto his servants; show yourselves in power, and make me a strong seething; for I am of Him that lives forever"[317]

The main female characters in *The Chemical Wedding of Christian Rosenkreutz*, one of the key defining Rosicrucian manuscripts, dating to the early seventeenth century CE, clearly parallel the different guises of the Shekinah. It is clearly no accident that the three female characters in the story correspond to the different manifestations of the Shekinah. The Old Queen in the tale, who is entirely focused on the spiritual and celestial matters is the Cosmic or Heavenly Shekinah. The Virgin corresponds to the Earthly Shekinah, and is the active principle, ensuring the sevenfold journey is accomplished by the worthy. Mediating between these is the Bride, corresponding to the Unified Shekinah, and her King thus correspondingly being God. That the two should play a

---

317 The Second Call, 1584

game similar to chess with the virtues and vices pitted against each other on the seventh and final day has clear Qabalistic and Merkavah overtones corresponding to the journey to the palace of the Heavenly Shekinah.

We briefly mentioned the Shekinah in connection with alchemy earlier in this work, and it is interesting to note that Sophia was mentioned in alchemical texts. She is praised in the early seventeenth century text *The Waterstone of the Wise*:

> "*Sophia (Wisdom), who is bright like Phoebus. Her body is naked because she is ardently loved. She is loved because she has at her disposal the riches of the whole world. He that gazes upon her beauteous form cannot refrain himself from loving her, goddess as she is.*"[318]

In the late seventeenth century text *On the Philadelphian (Spiritual) Gold*, the importance of Sophia is again mentioned with the line, "*For the Psyche in man is never able to penetrate beyond the image; only the pure spirit of Sophia can reach to the life*"[319]

In addition to magical texts, the period from the Renaissance through into the Industrial Age would see the Shekinah appearing in English religious texts, and also in poetry. In 1663 John Stillingfleet published *Shecinah: or a Demonstration of the Divine Presence in the Places of Religious Worship*, introducing her to the English language. Other writers took up the banner, such as George Hickes with his *The Moral Schechinah: or a Discourse on God's Glory* (1682) and J Scott describing "*That fiery Schechinah, or visible Glory of the Lord, in which he descended on Mount Sinai*".[320]

---

318 The Waterstone of the Wise, 1619.
319 A Conference betwixt Philocrysus and Philadelphus on the Philadelphian Gold, 1697.
320 Christian Life, Scott, 1681-86.

In an example of gender misappropriation the seventeenth century also saw the Shekinah being used as an alternative name for Jesus. This reached its apogee in the work of the Methodist hymnist Charles Wesley (1707-1788 CE), who wrote:

> *"Our Eyes on Earth survey*
> *The Dazzling Shechinah*
> *Bright, in endless Glory bright,*
> *Now in Flesh He stoops to dwell."*[321]

If a person was selective in their reading, they could choose to focus only on verses which seem to equate the Shekinah to Jesus in the *New Testament*. Thus in *2 Corinthians* it states,

> *"For it is the God who said, 'Let light shine out of darkness', who has shone in our hearts to give the light of the knowledge of the glory of God in the face of Jesus Christ."*[322]

However the terminology in this verse clearly does not equate the Shekinah to Jesus when taken in the correct context. The Shekinah is being referred to as the light which shone out of darkness (i.e. the primordial light), and also the light of the knowledge of the glory (i.e. kavod as the Shekinah) of God. This light shines in the face of Jesus, not from the face of Jesus, showing that he is being illuminated by the Shekinah, not radiating her power.

This type of selective quoting ignores the fact that Jesus was placed next to the Shekinah in the *Gospel of Luke*. When Jesus is on the mountain with Peter, John and James, and they behold him talking to Moses and Elijah, the Shekinah manifests as a cloud (c.f. the Sakina as a cloud in Islam discussed earlier).

---

321 Hymn on the Titles of Christ, Wesley, 1739.
322 2 Corinthians 4:6, C1st CE.

> *"While he was saying this, a cloud came and overshadowed them; and they were terrified as they entered the cloud. Then from the cloud came a voice that said, 'This is my Son, my Beloved; listen to him!'"*[323]

The connection between Jesus and the Shekinah is further emphasised in *1 Peter*, where it states:

> *"If you are reviled for the name of Christ, you are blessed, because the spirit of glory [the Shekinah], which is the Spirit of God, is resting on you."*[324]

If men could try and misappropriate the Shekinah, women too could write about her, as seen in the writings of Mary Anne Evans (1819-1880 CE) under her pen name of George Eliot:

> *"The golden sunlight beamed through the dripping boughs like a Shechinah, or visible divine presence."*[325]

Moving into the early twentieth century, The Fellowship of the Rose Cross, founded in 1915, was one of the splinter groups formed out of the ashes of the Hermetic Order of the Golden Dawn, the prominent magical order founded in 1888 which had fragmented in 1900-1903. The prime mover in this splinter order was the prolific author and mystic Arthur Edward Waite (1857-1942 CE).

It was undoubtedly due to Waite's influence that the Shekinah features heavily in many of the initiation rituals of the Fellowship of the Rose Cross. She is also found by name or titles and other references in the Equinox Ritual and Solstice Rituals of the same order. In the Adeptus

---

323 Luke 9:34-35, C1st-C2nd CE.
324 1 Peter 4:14, C1st-C2nd CE.
325 Scenes of Clerical Life, Eliot, 1856.

Exemptus (7=4) initiation ritual, the following line spoken by the priest is indicative of the flavour of the Shekinah in these ceremonies:

> *"Be thou blessed by the mouth of Shekinah in all thy grades and degrees, in all the Sephiroth which have been sanctified and exalted in thee."*[326]

An increase of interest in the Shekinah has gone hand in hand with the resurgence of interest in the divine feminine in recent decades, as demonstrated by the corresponding increase in academic and theological research. In recent years the Shekinah has also become more prominent through the work of such organisations as the Jewish Renewal Movement in America, which merges the mystical nature of the Shekinah with some of the more orthodox teachings of Judaism.[327]

Through this snapshot of some of the significant esoteric writings of recent centuries it is clear that the influence of the Shekinah has expanded into many other branches of the esoteric revival. This has been assisted by the increase in availability of source materials dealing both directly and indirectly with the Shekinah, as well as a blossoming interest in the divine feminine.

---

326 Adeptus Exemptus (7=4) Initiation Ritual, Fellowship of the Rosy Cross, 1916:37.
327 See Meanings of Shekhinah in the Jewish Renewal Movement, Weissler, 2005

# Wisdom

As we have demonstrated throughout this work, there is clearly a direct line of descent from the Canaanite goddess Asherah to the Wisdom Goddess, and thence to the Shekinah and Sophia. Additionally we can see that the Shekinah and her qualities influenced perceptions of the Holy Spirit and the Virgin Mary in Christianity, and the Sakina in Islam.

The extent to which earlier goddesses like the Sumerian Inanna and Egyptian Isis-Ma'at influenced the development of the Shekinah is difficult to determine, and at this point we will simply draw attention to the similarity between some of their motifs and those associated with Asherah and the Shekinah as a possible (or indeed probable) indication of influence.

Having explored the possible roots of the Shekinah, contemporary wisdom goddesses and possible and likely derivatives, it is clear that she represents an enduring motif throughout history, which speaks to something in the human spirit. Although the Shekinah is most present as a named figure in the literature of the Kabbalah and Merkavah Mysticism, it is clear from these writings that the Kabbalists, Rabbis and Mystics writing about her in the Middle Ages and Renaissance considered her to be the same as the unnamed Wisdom Goddess of early Jewish wisdom literature, including the *Book of Proverbs* in the *Old Testament.*

The cross-fertilisation between the Shekinah and Sophia is a clear example of how different manifestations can arise from the same sources acted upon by different influences, as both developed from early wisdom literature. In the case of the Shekinah these influences can be seen to include the Canaanite, Egyptian, and Sumerian/Babylonian cultures, whereas Sophia was more heavily influenced by Hellenic, Jewish and Christian cultures. In this Sophia may be seen as being the more derivative from the other, as the Jewish culture which produced the Shekinah also influenced the development of Sophia.

The numerous parallels and interconnections between the Shekinah and Sophia are seen in many of texts. As the divine feminine wisdom and world soul, the primordial light of creation, the words from a Gnostic text below could equally be describing the Shekinah, and her role in the world:

> "I am the Womb that gives shape to the All by giving birth to the Light that shines in splendour. I am the Aeon to come. I am the fulfilment of the All, that is, Meirothea, the glory of the Mother."[328]

The cross-fertilisation of the Shekinah and Sophia also undoubtedly contributed to their influence on the development of Christian literature, seen clearly in early sources as well as medieval and later writings. The increase in scope and detail of information provided about the Shekinah in the Kabbalah reflects an increase in interest in her, which may be a reflection of her being seen as the Shabbat Bride of Judaism.

The Shabbat Bride is an essential part of Judaism, and the great medieval Kabbalist Isaac Luria (1534-1572 CE) wrote a beautiful *Hymn to the Shekinah for the Feast of the Sabbath* (translation included by kind permission of Jerome Rothenberg), with which we will end this work:

---

328  Trimorphic Protennoia, C4th CE, trans. J.D. Turner.

# Hymn to the Shekinah
# for the Feast of the Sabbath

Isaac Luria, translated by Jerome Rothenberg

*I have sung*
*an old measure*
*would open*
*gates to*
*her field of apples*
*(each one a power)*
*set a new table*
*to feed her*
*& beautifully*
*candelabrum*
*drops its*
*light on us*
*Between right & left*
*the Bridge*
*draws near in*
*holy jewels*
*clothes of the Sabbath*
*whose lover*
*embraces her*
*down to foundation*
*gives pleasure*
*squeezes his strength out*
*in surcease of*
*sorrow*
*& makes new faces*
*be hers*
*& new souls*
*new breath*
*gives her joy*
*double measure*
*of lights & of*
*streams for her blessing*

*O Friends of the Bride*
*go forth*
*give her many*
*sweet foods to taste*
*many kinds of*
*fish*
*for fertility*
*birth*
*of new souls*
*new spirits*
*will follow the 32 paths*
*& 3 branches*
*the Bride with*
*70 crowns*
*with her King who*
*hovers above her*
*crown above crown in*
*Holy of Holies*
*this lady all worlds are*
*formed in*
*all's sealed*
*within her*
*shines forth from*
*Ancient of Days*
*Toward the south*
*I have placed*
*candelabrum*
*(o mystical)*
*room in*
*the north*
*for table*
*for bread*
*for pitchers of wine*

*for sweet myrtle*
*gives power to*
*lovers*
*new potencies*
*garlands*
*of words for her*
*70 crowns*
*50 gates*
*the Shekinah*
*ringed by*
*6 loaves*
*of the Sabbath*
*& bound*
*all sides to*
*Heavenly Refuge*
*the impure powers*
*have gone*
*demons you feared sleep*
*in chains*

# Bibliography

Abma, Richtsje (1999) *Bonds of Love: Methodic Studies of Prophetic Texts with Marriage Imagery.* Assen, Uitgeverij van Gorcum

Ackerman, Susan (1999) *And the Women Knead Dough: The Worship of the Queen of Heaven in Sixth Century Judah.* In *Women in the Hebrew Bible: A Reader* by Alice Bach (ed). London, Routledge

Ackerman, Susan (1993) *The Queen Mother and the Cult in Ancient Israel.* In *Journal of Biblical Literature* Vol 112:385-401

Ameisenowa, Zofia (1949) *Animal-Headed Gods, Evangelists, Saints and Righteous Men.* In *Journal of the Warburg and Courtauld Institutes* Vol 12:21-45

Arbel, Vita Daphna (2003) *Beholders of Divine Secrets. Mysticism and Myth in the Hekhalot and Merkavah Literature.* New York, SUNY Press

Abulafia, Abraham (2007) *Get Ha-Shemot – Divorce of the Names.* Rhode Island, Providence University

Altmann, Alexander (1969) *Studies in Religious Philosophy and Mysticism.* New York, Ithaca

Apuleius, Lucius & Adlington, William (trans) (1996) *The Golden Ass.* Ware, Wordsworth

Athanassiadi, Polymnia, & Frede, Michael (eds) (1999) *Pagan Monotheism in Late Antiquity.* Oxford, Oxford University Press

Aubet, Maria Eugenia (2001) *The Phoenicians and the West: Politics, Colonies and Trade*. Cambridge, Cambridge University Press

Bach, Alice (ed) (1999) *Women in the Hebrew Bible: A Reader*. London, Routledge

Barnstone, Willis & Meyer, Marvin (2003) *The Gnostic Bible: Gnostic Texts of Mystical Wisdom from the Ancient and Medieval Worlds*. London, Shambala Publications

Beale, Gregory K. (1999) *The Book of Revelation: a Commentary on the Greek Text*. Michigan, Wm B. Erdmanns Publishing

Beck, E. (1979) *Ephraem Syrus. Sermones in Hebdomadam Sanctam. Syr. 182*. Leuven, Peeters

Benko, Stephen (2003) *The Virgin Goddess: Studies in the Pagan and Christian Roots of Mariology*. Leiden, Brill

Betz, Hans Dieter (ed) (1996) *The Greek Magical Papyri in Translation*. Chicago, University of Chicago Press

Binger, Tilde (1997) *Asherah: Goddesses in Ugarit, Israel and the Old Testament*. London, Sheffield Academic Press

Blau, J.L. (1944) *The Christian Interpretation of the Cabala in the Renaissance*. Columbia, Columbia University Press

Bonner, Campbell (1949) *An Amulet of the Ophite Gnostics*. In *Hesperia Supplements* Vol 8:43-46+444

Bonnet, C. (1996) *Astarté: dossier documentaire et perspectives historiques*. Rome, Consiglio Nazionale delle Ricerce.

Boustan, Ra'anan S., & Reed, Annette Yoshiko (eds) (2004) *Heavenly Realms and Earthly Realities in Late Antique Religions*. Cambridge, Cambridge University Press

Box, G.H. (1932) *The Idea of Intermediation in Jewish Theology. A Note on Memra and Shekinah*. In *The Jewish Quarterly Review* Vol 23.2:103-119

British Museum (1921) *The Babylonian Legends of the Creation*. London, Harrison & Sons Ltd

Budin, Stephanie L. (2004) *A reconsideration of the Aphrodite-Ashtart Syncretism*. In *Numen* Vol. 51:95-145

Buxbaum, Yitzhak (1995) *Jewish Spiritual Practices*. Maryland, Jacob Aronson

Carter, Jane Burr (1987) *The Masks of Ortheia.* In *American Journal of Archaeology* Vol 91.3:355-383

Clifford, Richard J. (1971) *The Tent of El and the Israelite Tent of Meeting.* In *Catholic Biblical Quarterly* Vol 33:221-227.

Cohn, Herbert (2004) *Is the "Queen of Heaven" in Jeremiah the Goddess Anat.* In *Jewish Bible Quarterly,* Vol 32.1:55-57

Connor, Miguel (ed.) (2011) *Voices of Gnosticism.* Dublin, Bardic Press

Conybeare, F.C. (1898) *The Testament of Solomon.* In *The Jewish Quarterly Review* Vol II.1:2-45

Corbin, Henry (1986) *Temple and Contemplation.* London, KPI Ltd

Cornelius, Izak (1994) *The Iconography of the Canaanite Gods Reshef and Baal: Late Bronze and Iron Age Periods.* Göttingen, Vandenhoeck & Ruprecht

Cross, Frank Moore (1997) *Canaanite Myth and Hebrew Epic: Essays in the History of the Religion of Israel.* Harvard, Harvard University Press

Cross, Frank Moore (1962) *Yahweh and the God of the Patriarchs.* In *Harvard Theological Review* Vol. 55.4:225-259

Dan, Joseph (ed) (1986) *The Early Kabbalah.* New Jersey, Paulist Press

Dan, Joseph, & Herrmann, Klaus, & Petzoldt, Manuela (1999) *Studies in Jewish Manuscripts.* Tubingen, Mohr Siebeck

Day, John (2002) *Yahweh and the Gods and Goddesses of Canaan.* Sheffield, Sheffield Academic Press Ltd

Day, John (1986) *Asherah in the Hebrew Bible and Northwest Semitic Literature.* In *Journal of Biblical Literature* 105.3:385-408

Day, John, & Gordon, Robert P., & Williamson, Hugh G.M. (eds) (1997) *Wisdom in Ancient Israel.* Cambridge, Cambridge University Press

De Manhar, Nurho (2008) *The Sepher Ha-Zohar.* Charleston, BiblioBazaar LLC

Dennis, Rabbi Geoffrey W. (2007) *The Encyclopedia of Jewish Myth, Magic and Mysticism.* Minnesota, Llewellyn

D'Este, Sorita (ed) (2010) *Hekate Her Sacred Fires*. London, Avalonia

D'Este, Sorita & Rankine, D. (2009) *Hekate Liminal Rites*. London, Avalonia

D'Este, Sorita & Rankine, D. (2009) *Practical Elemental Magick*. London, Avalonia

D'Este, Sorita & Rankine, D. (2008) *The Isles of the Many Gods*. London, Avalonia

D'Este, Sorita (2005) *Artemis – Virgin Goddess of the Sun and Moon*. London, Avalonia

Deutsch, Nathaniel (1999) *Guardians of the Gate: Angelic Vice Regency in Late Antiquity*. Leiden, Brill

Deutsch, Nathaniel (1995) *The Gnostic Imagination: Gnosticism, Mandaeism and Merkabah Mysticism*. Leiden, Brill

Dever, William G. (2005) *Did God Have a Wife? Archaeology and Folk Religion in Ancient Israel*. Cambridge, Wm. B. Erdmanns Publishing Co

Donner, H. & Röllig, W. (eds) (2000) *Kanaanäische und Aramäische Inscriften*. Wiesbaden, Harrassowitz.

Elior, Rachel (2004) *The Three Temples: On the Emergence of Jewish Mysticism*. Oxford, Littmann

Etheridge, J.W. (2005) *The Targum of Onkelos And Jonathan Ben Uzziel on the Pentateuch I: Genesis And Exodus*. New Jersey, Gorgias Press

Fallon, Francis T. (1978) *The Enthronement of Sabaoth: Jewish Elements in Gnostic Creation Myths*. Leiden, Brill

Faraone, Christopher A. & Emily Teeter (2004) *Egyptian Maat and Hesiodic Metis*. In *Mnemosyne* Fourth Series, Vol 57 Fasc 2:177-208

Firestone, Reuven (1999) *Journeys in Holy Lands: the Evolution of the Abraham-Ishamel Legends in Islamic Exegesis*. New York, SUNY

Fischer-Rizzi, Susanne (1998) *The Complete Incense Book*. New York, Sterling Publishing Company

Fontaine, Carole R. (1981) *The Instruction of Ptahhotep Revisited*. In *Bible Archaeologist* Vol. 44.3:155-160

Fröhlich, Isa, (2010) *Theology and Demonology in Qumran Texts*. In *Henoch*:101-129

Gaster, Moses (1971) *Studies and Texts in Folklore, Magic, Medieval Romance, Hebrew Apocrypha and Samaritan Archaeology*. New Jersey, KTAV

Gaster, Moses (1893) *Hebrew Visions of Hell and Paradise*. In *Journal of the Royal Asiatic Society of Great Britain and Ireland*, July 1893:571-611

Gero, Stephen (1976) *The Spirit as a Dove at the Baptism of Jesus*. In *Novum Testamentum* Vol 18:17-35

Gilmour, Garth (2009) *An Iron Age II Pictorial Inscription from Jerusalem Illustrating Yahweh and Asherah*. In *Palestine Exploration Quarterly* Vol. 141.2:87-103

Ginsburg, Christian D. (1970) *The Kabbalah, its Doctrines, Development and Literature*. London, Routledge

Ginsburg, Elliot Kiba (1989) *The Sabbath in the Classical Kabbalah*. New York, SUNY

Ginzberg, Louis (1970) *On Jewish Law and Lore*. New York, Atheneum

Ginzberg, Louis (1909) *The Legends of the Jews*. Philadelphia, Jewish Publication Society

Gnuse, Robert Karl (1997) *No Other Gods: Emergent Monotheism in Israel.* London, Continuum International Publishing Group

Godwin, Joscelyn (trans), & McLean, Adam (intro) (1991) *The Chemical Wedding of Christian Rosenkreutz*. Michigan, Phanes Press

Goehring, James E. (1981) *A Classical Influence on the Gnostic Sophia Myth*. In *Vigiliae Christianae* Vol 35.1:16-23

Goldman, Norman Saul (1978) *Rabbinic Theology and the Unconscious*. In *Journal of Religion and Health* Vol 17.2:144-150

Good, Deidre J. (1987) *Reconstructing the Tradition of Sophia in Gnostic Literature*. Georgia, Scholars Press

Green, Arthur (1997) *Kether: The Crown of God in Early Jewish Mysticism.* Princeton, Princeton University Press

Grigson, Geoffrey (1978) *The Goddess of Love. The Birth, Triumph, Death and Return of Aphrodite*. London, Quartet Books

Gruenwald, Ithamar (1980) *Apocalyptic & Merkavah Mysticism.* Leiden, Brill

Hadley, Judith M. (2000) *The Cult of Asherah in ancient Israel and Judah: evidence for a Hebrew Goddess.* Cambridge, Cambridge University Press

Haibach- Reinisch, Monika (1962) *Ein Neuer 'Transitus Mariae' des Pseudo-Melito.* Vatican City, Pontifica Academia Mariana Internationalis

Hayman, Peter (1984) *Some Observations on Sefer Yesira (1) Its use of Scripture.* In *Journal of Jewish Studies* Vol. 35:164-184

Holland, Frederick, & Kuntz, Darcy (ed) (2009) *The Revelation of the Shechinah or the Tree of Life in the Holy Royal Arch.* Texas, Golden Dawn Research Trust (originally 1887)

Hornung, Erik (1996) *Conceptions of God in Ancient Egypt. The One and the Many.* New York, Cornell University Press

Idel, Moshe (1990) *Kabbalah: New Perspectives.* Connecticut, Yale University Press

Idel, Moshe (1986) *The Early Kabbalah.* New Jersey, Paulist Press

Isaacs, Ronald H. (1997) *Ascending Jacob's Ladder: Jewish Views of Angels, Demons and Evil Spirits.* Maryland, Rowman & Littlefield

Jackson, Bernard S. (1992) *The Prophet and the Law in Early Judaism and the New Testament.* In *Cardozo Studies in Law and Literature* 4.2:123-166

Jackson, Howard M. (1989) *The Origin in Ancient Incantatory "Voces Magicae" of Some Names in the Sethian Gnostic System.* In *Vigiliae Christianae* Vol 43.1:69-79

James, Edwin Oliver (1996) *The Tree of Life. An Archaeological Study.* Leiden, Brill

James, M.R. (1924) *The Apocryphal New Testament.* Oxford, Clarendon Press

Janowitz, Naomi (2002) *Icons of Power: Ritual Practices in Late Antiquity.* Pennsylvania, Pennsylvania State University Press

Jowettt, B. (1892) *The Dialogues of Plato translated into English with Analyses and Introductions* (5 volumes). Oxford, Oxford University Press

Julian of Norwich & Holloway, J.B. (2003) *Showing of Love*. Minnesota, Liturgical Press

Kadushin, Max (2001) *The Rabbinic Mind*. New York, Global Academic Publishing

Kanarfogel, Ephraim (2000) *Peering Through the Lattices. Mystical, Magical, and Pietistic Dimensions in the Tosafist Period*. Detroit, Wayne State University Press

Kaplan, Aryeh (1997) *Sefer Yetzirah. The Book of Creation*. Maine, Weiser

Kaplan, Aryeh (1982) *Meditation and Kabbalah*. Maine, Weiser

Kaplan, Aryeh (1981) *The Living Torah* (5 volumes). New York, Moznaim Publishing Corporation

Kaplan, Aryeh (1979) *The Bahir Illumination*. Maine, Weiser

Kaplan, Aryeh (1985) *Jewish Meditation*. New York, Schocken Books

Karenga, Maulana (2004) *Maat: The Moral Ideal in Ancient Egypt*. London, Routledge

Keel, Othmar, & Uehlinger, Christoph (2001) *Gods, Goddesses and Images of God in Ancient Israel*. London, Continuum International Publishing Group

Kerényi, C. (1951) *The Gods of the Greeks*. London, Thames & Hudson

King, Georgiana G. (1933) *Some Reliefs at Budapest*. In *American Journal of Archaeology* Vol 37.1:64-76

Kingsley, Peter (1995) *Ancient Philosophy, Mystery, and Magic. Empedocles and the Pythagorean Tradition*. Oxford, Oxford University Press

Kloppenborg, John S. (1982) *Isis and Sophia in the Book of Wisdom*. In *Harvard Theological Review* Vol. 75.1:57-84

Kornblatt, Judith Deutsch (1991) *Solov'ev's Androgynous Sophia and the Jewish Kabbalah*. In *Slavic Review* 50.3:487-496

Lambert, W.G. (1982) *Hymn to the Queen of Nippur*. In *Zikir Sumin*, Uitgeverij, pp173-218

Lanner, Laurel (2006) *Who will lament her? The feminine and the fantastic in the book of Nahum.* London, Continuum International Publishing Group

Laycock, Donald, & Skinner, Stephen (1978) *The Complete Enochian Dictionary.* London, Askin Publishers

Lenzi, Alan (2006) *Proverbs 8:22-31 – Three Perspectives on Its Composition.* In *Journal of Biblical Literature* Vol. 125.4:687-714

Lesses, Rebecca Macy (1997) *Ritual Practices to Gain Power. Angels, Incantations, and Revelation in Early Jewish Mysticism.* Texas, Trinity Press International

Lesses, Rebecca Macy (1996) *Speaking with Angels: Jewish and Greco-Egyptian Revelatory Adjurations.* In *Harvard Theological Review* Vol. 89:41-60

Lindenberger, James M. (2003) *Ancient Aramaic and Hebrew Letters.* Atlanta, Society of Biblical Literature

Lobel, Diana (1999) *A Dwelling Place for the Shekinah.* In *The Jewish Quarterly Review* Vol 90.1/2:103-125

Lovelock, James (2000) *Gaia: A New Look at Life on Earth.* Oxford, Oxford University Press (3rd edition)

Lutzky, Harriet (1998) *Shadday as a Goddess Epithet.* In *Vetus Testamentum* Vol. 48.1:15-36

Luzatto, Rabbi Moses (1970) *General Principles of Kabbalah.* Jerusalem, Research Centre of Kabbalah Press

Mack, Burton L. (1970) *Wisdom Myth and Mytho-logy.* In *Interpretation* Vol. 24.1:46-60

MacRae, George W. (1970) *The Jewish Background of the Gnostic Sophia Myth.* In *Novum Testamentum* Vol 12.2:86-101

Marcovich, Miroslav (1996) *From Ishtar To Aphrodite.* In *Journal of Aesthetic Education* Vol 30.2:43-59

Marcovich, Miroslav (1988) *The Wedding Hymn of Acta Thomae.* In *Studies in Graeco-Roman Religions and Gnosticism.* Leiden, Brill

Marinatos, Nannó (2000) *The Goddess and the Warrior: the Naked Goddess and Mistress of Animals in Early Greek Religion.* London, Routledge

Marsman, Hennie J. (2003) *Women in Ugarit and Israel: Their Social and Religious Position in the Context if the Ancient Near East.* Leiden, Brill

Mastin, B.A. (2009) *The Inscriptions Written on Plaster at Kuntillet 'Ajrud.* In *Vetus Testamentum* Vol. 59:99-115

Mathers, S.L. MacGregor (1912) *The Kabbalah Unveiled.* New York, Theosophical Publishing Co.

Matt, Daniel Chanan (2003-2009) *The Zohar, Pritzker Edition* (5 vols). Chicago, Stanford University Press

Matt, Daniel Chanan (1983) *Zohar, the Book of Enlightenment.* London, Paulist Press

Matt, Daniel Chanan (1980) *David ben Yehudah Hehasid and his Book of Mirrors.* In *Hebrew Union College Annual* 51:129-172

Mead, G.R.S. (1921) *Pistis Sophia: A Gnostic Gospel.* London, J.M. Watkins

Mead, G.R.S. (1900) *Fragments of a Faith Forgotten.* London, Theosophical Publishing Society

Meador, Betty De Shong (2000) *Inanna, Lady of Largest Heart. Poems of the Sumerian High Priestess Enheduanna.* Texas, University of Texas Press

Meltzer, David (ed) (1976) *The Secret Garden: An Anthology in the Kabbalah.* New York, Seabury Press

Menes, Abraham (1947-8) *The Ethical Teachings of Moses Hayim Luzatto.* In *Proceedings of the American Academy for Jewish Research* Vol 17:61-68

Metzger, Bruce M. (ed) (1991) *The Holy Bible: New Revised Standard Version with Apocrypha.* Oxford, Oxford University Press

Meyer, Marvin W., & Smith, Richard (1999) *Ancient Christian Magic. Coptic Texts of Ritual Power.* Princeton, Princeton University Press

Middleton, R.D. (1938) *Logos and Shekinah in the Fourth Gospel.* In *The Jewish Quarterly Review* 29(2):101-133

Munk, Linda (1992) *His Dazzling Absence: The Shekinah in Jonathan Edwards.* In *Early American Literature* 27.1:1-30

Murphy, Roland Edmund (2002) *The Tree of Life: an Exploration of Biblical Wisdom Literature.* Cambridge, Wm. B. Eerdmanns

Murray, Robert (1975) *Symbols of Church and Kingdom: a Study in Early Syriac Tradition.* Cambridge, Cambridge University Press

Naveh, Joseph, & Shaked, Shaul (1998) *Amulets and Magic Bowls. Aramaic Incantations of Late Antiquity.* Jerusalem, Magnes Press

Naveh, Joseph & Shaked, Shaul (1993) *Magic Spells and Formulae: Aramaic Incantations of Late Antiquity.* Jerusalem, Magnes Press

Newman, Barbara (1997) *Sister of Wisdom: St Hildegard's Theology of the Feminine.* California, University of California Press

Newman, Barbara (ed) (1988) *Saint Hildegard of Bingen: Symphonia. A Critical Edition of the Symphonia armonie celestium revelationum.* New York, Cornell University Press

Newman, Louis I. (1978) *Talmudic Anthology: Tales and Teachings of the Rabbis.* New Jersey, Behrmann House Publishing

Nielsen, Kjeld (1986) *Incense in Ancient Israel.* Leiden, Brill

Noll, K.I. (2008) *Was there Doctrinal Dissemination in Early Yahweh Religion?* In *Biblical Interpretation* 16:395-427

Oehler, Gust Fr. (2009) *Theology of the Old Testament.* Charleston, Bibliolife

Olyan, Saul M. (1988) *Asherah and the Cult of Yahweh in Israel.* Atlanta, Scholars Press

Padeh, Zwe & Menzi, D.W. (1999) *The Palace of Adam Kadmon.* Jerusalem, Jason Aronson Inc

Parisinou, Eva (2000) *The Light of the Gods: The Role of Light in Archaic and Classical Greek Cult.* London, Duckworth

Parpola, Simo (1993) *The Assyrian Tree of Life: Tracing the Origins of Jewish Monotheism and Greek Philosophy.* In *Journal of Near Eastern Studies* Vol 53(4):161-208

Parpola, S. & Watanabe, K. (1988) *Neo-Assyrian Treaties and Loyalty Oaths.* Helsinki, Helsinki University Press.

Patai, Raphael (1990) *The Hebrew Goddess.* Detroit, Wayne State University Press

Patai, Raphael (1965) *The Goddess Asherah.* In *Journal of Near Eastern Studies* Vol 24(1):37-52

Patai, Raphael (1964) *Lilith.* In *The Journal of American Folklore* Vol 77.306:295-314

Penchansky, David (2005) *Twilight of the Gods: Polytheism in the Hebrew Bible.* Kentucky, Westminster John Knox Press

Peters, Francis E. (1990) *Judaism, Christianity, and Islam: the Classical Texts and Their Interpretation.* Princeton, Princeton University Press

Pinch, Geraldine (2002) *Egyptian Mythology.* Oxford, Oxford University Press

Plotinus (1991) *The Enneads.* London, Penguin Books

Ponce, Charles (1974) *Kabbalah.* London, Garnstone Press

Quispel, G. (1975) *Jewish Gnosis and Mandaean Gnosticism.* In *Les Textes de Nag Hammadi.* Leiden, Brill

Rankine, David, & d'Este, Sorita (2009) *Practical Qabalah Magick.* London, Avalonia

Rankine, David, & D'Este, Sorita (2007) *The Isles of the Many Gods.* London, Avalonia

Rankine, David (2006) *Heka. The Practices of Ancient Egyptian Ritual and Magic.* London, Avalonia

Rankine, David (2005) *Climbing the Tree of Life.* London, Avalonia

Rayment, Collette (1997) *The Shapeliness of the Shekinah: Structural Unity in the Thought of Peter Steele SJ.* PhD Thesis, Sydney University

Ritner, R.K. (1993) *The Mechanics of Ancient Egyptian Magical Practice.* Chicago, Studies in Oriental Civilization 54

Robinson, J.M. (ed) (1977) *The Nag Hammadi Library in English.* New York, Harper & Row

Ronan, Stephen (ed) (1992) *The Goddess Hekate.* Hastings, Chthonios Books

Roussel, P. & Launey, M. (1937) *Inscriptions de Delos.* Paris, Honore Champion

Savedow, Steve (ed, trans) (2000) *Sepher Rezial Hemelach. The Book of the Angel Rezial.* Maine, Samuel Weiser Inc

Schaeffer, C.F.A. (1939) *Ugaritica V: Panthéon d'Ugarit.* Paris, Geuthner.

Schäfer, Peter (2002) *Mirror Of His Beauty. Feminine Images of God from the Bible to the Early Kabbalah.* Princeton, Princeton University Press

Schäfer, Peter (1992) *The Hidden and Manifest God. Some Major Themes in Early Jewish Mysticism.* New York, SUNY

Scheinkin, David (1986) *Path of Kabbalah.* London, Continuum International Publishing Group

Scholem, Gershom (1991) *On the Mystical Shape of the Godhead.* New York, Schocken

Scholem, Gershom (1990) *Origins of the Kabbalah.* Princeton, Princeton Paperbacks

Scholem, Gershom (1969) *Major Trends in Jewish Mysticism.* New York, Schocken

Scholem, Gershom (1965) *On the Kabbalah and Its Symbolism.* New York, Schocken

Scholem, Gershom (1965) *Jewish Gnosticism Merkavah Mysticism and Talmudic Tradition.* New York, Jewish Theological Seminary of America

Scholem, Gershom (1949) *Zohar. The Book of Splendour.* New York, Schocken Books

Schrire, Theodor (1966) *Hebrew Amulets.* London, Routledge & Kegan Paul

Schwartz, Dov (2005) *Studies on Astral Magic in Medieval Jewish Thought.* Leiden, Brill

Schwartz, Eduard (ed) (1927) *Acta Conciliorum Oecumenicorum.* New York, Walter de Gruyter

Scopello, Madeleine (1980) *The Apocalypse of Zostrianos (Nag Hammadi VIII .1) and the Book of the Secrets of Enoch.* In *Vigilae Christianae* Vol 34.4:376-385

Shaked, Shaul (2006) *Dramatis Personae in the Jewish Magical Texts: Some Differences between Incantation Bowls and Geniza Magic.* In *Jewish Studies Quarterly* 13:363-387

Shaked, Shaul (ed) (2005) *Officina Magica. Essays on the Practice of Magic in Antiquity.* Leiden, Brill

Skinner, Stephen & Rankine, David (2007) *The Goetia of Dr Rudd.* Singapore, Golden Hoard Press

0

# Bibliography

Skipworth, Grey Hubert (1906) *Ashtoreth, the Goddess of the Zidonians*. Jewish Quarterly Review Vol 18.4:715-738

Smith, Margaret (1984) *Rabi'a The Mystic and her Fellow-Saints in Islam: Being the Life and Teachings of Rabi'a al-Adawiyya Al-Qaysiyya of Basra together with some account of the place of the Women Saints in Islam*. Cambridge, Cambridge University Press

Smith, Mark S. (2002) *The Early History of God: Yahweh and the Other Deities in Ancient Israel*. Cambridge, Wm B Eerdmanns Publishing

Smith, Morton (trans) & Karr, Don (ed) (2009) *Hekhalot Rabbati. The Greater Treatise Concerning the Palaces of Heaven*.

Sperling, Harry, & Simon, Maurice (trans) (1933) *The Zohar* (5 volumes). London, Soncino Press

Stavish, Mark. (2007) *Freemasonry: Rituals, Symbols & History of the Secret Society*. Minnesota, Llewellyn

Stead, G.C. (1969) *The Valentinian Myth of Sophia*. In *Journal of Theological Studies* Vol. 20.1:75-104

Strong, Herbert A., & Garstang, John (trans) (1913) *The Syrian Goddess*. London, Constable & Co

Stuckenbruck, Loren T. (1995) *Angel Veneration and Christology. A Study in Early Judaism and in the Christology of the Apocalypse of John*. Tubingen, Mohr Siebeck

Swartz, Michael D. (1996) *Scholastic Magic: Ritual and Revelation in Early Jewish Mysticism*. Princeton, Princeton University Press

Swartz, Michael D. (1992) *Mystical Prayer in Early Jewish Mysticism: An Analysis of Ma'aseh Merkavah*. Tubingen, Mohr Siebeck

Taylor, J. Glen (1982) *The Song of Deborah and Two Canaanite Goddesses*. In *Journal for the Study of the Old Testament* Vol. 23:99-108

Thorndike, Lynn (1923) *History of Magic and Experiment Science Vol 1. The first Thirteen Centuries*. Columbia, Columbia University Press

Tigunait, Pandit Rajmani. (1998) *Śakti: The Power in Tanta. A Scholarly Approach*. Pennsylvania, The Himalayan Institute Press

Trachtenberg, Joshua (1939) *Jewish Magic and Superstition.* New Jersey, Behrman House

Tubbs, Jonathan N. (1999) *Canaanites.* Oklahoma, University of Oklahoma Press

Turner, John D. (1980) *The Gnostic Threefold Path to Enlightenment: The Ascent of Mind and the Descent of Wisdom.* In *Novum Testamentum* Vol 22.4:324-351

Ulrich, E. (2004) *Our Sharper Focus on the Bible and Theology Thanks to the Dead Sea Scrolls.* In *Catholic Biblical Quarterly* Vol. 66:1-24

Vance, Donald R. (1994) *Literary Sources for the History of Palestine and Syria: The Phoenician Inscriptions.* In *The Bible Archaeologist* Vol 57.2:110-120

Van Den Broek, Roelof (2003) *Gospel Tradition and Salvation in Justin the Gnostic.* In *Vigiliae Christianae* Vol 57.4:363-388

Van Den Broek, Roelof (1973) *The Shape of Edem According to Justin the Gnostic.* In *Vigiliae Christianae* Vol 27.1:35-45

Van der Toorn, Karel (1992) *Anat-Yahu, Some Other Deities, and the Jews of Elephantine.* In *Numen* Vol 39.1:80-101

Verman, Mark. (1996) *The History and Varieties of Jewish Meditation.* Maryland, Jacob Aronson

Vital, Chaim. (2006) *Shaarei Kedusha – Gates of Holiness.* Rhode Island, Providence University

Waite, A.E. (1965) *The Holy Kabbalah.* New York, University Books

Waldstein, Michael, & Wisse, Frederick (ed) (1995) *The Apocryphon of John: Synopsis of Nag Hammadi Codices II.1. III.1; and IV.1 with BG 8502.2.* Leiden, Brill

Weissler, Chava (2005) *Meanings of Shekinah in the Jewish Renewal Movement.* In *Nashim,* Fall 2005.10:53-83

Welburn, Andrew (ed) (1998) *Mani, the Angel and the Column of Glory. An Anthology of Manichean Texts.* Edinburgh, Floris Books

Westcott, Wynn (ed) (1895) *The Chaldean Oracles of Zoroaster.* London, Theosophical Publishing Society

Wilkinson, Richard H. (2003) *The Complete Gods and Goddesses of Ancient Egypt.* London, Thames & Hudson

Winfield, Moshe (1996) *Feminine Features in the Imagery of God in Israel: The Sacred Marriage and the Sacred Tree.* In *Vetus Testamentum* Vol 46.4:515-529

Wolfson, Elliot (1994) *Through a Speculum That Shines: Vision and Imagination in Medieval Jewish Mysticism.* Princeton, Princeton University Press

Wolkstein, Diane, & Kramer, Samuel Noah (1984) *Inanna: Queen of Heaven and Earth.* London, Rider & Company

Wyatt, N. (2002) *Religious Texts From Ugarit.* London, Sheffield Academic Press Ltd

Yamauchi, Edwin M. (1978) *The Descent of Ishtar, the Fall of Sophia, and the Jewish Roots of Gnosticism.* In *Tyndale Bulletin* 29:143-175

Yamauchi, Edwin M. (1961) *Cultic Clues in Canticles?* In *Bulletin of the Evangelical Theological Society,* Vol. 4.3:80-88

Zevit, Ziony (2003) *The Religions of Ancient Israel: a Synthesis of Parallactic Approaches.* London, Continuum International Publishing Group

# Index

Dove, 23, 24, 25, 26, 111
Dumuzi, 68
Dybbuk, 182

# E

Eagle, 79, 105, 166
*Ecclesiastes*, 15, 79, 80
Echidna, 23, 104
Edem, 15, 23, 50, 76, 94,
 103, 104, 113
Eden, 11, 23, 30, 43, 45, 46,
 47, 98, 103, 113, 127,
 146, 148, 166
Egypt, 10, 39, 40, 41, 43,
 52, 57, 58, 66, 67, 68, 70,
 71, 73, 86, 87, 88, 125
El, 37, 58, 59, 60, 92, 133,
 136, 138, 139, 142
Elat, 59, *See* Asherah
Eleazer of Worms, 17, 47,
 49, 156
Elephantine, 53, 88
Elijah, 57
Elion, 55, 131, 139
Elioun, 131
*Elohim*, 53, 55, 103, 104,
 137, 139, 142, 144
Emerald Tablet, 47
Empedocles, 15, 43
Enheduanna, 14, 90
Enki, 37, 78, 80
Ennoia, 16, 72, 97, 98
Enoch, 128
Ephraim Ben Gershon, 18,
 150
Eros, 180
Eve, 14, 16, 22, 45, 47, 48,
 84, 102, 104, 113, 146,
 148, 153, 181
*Exodus*, 9, 14, 27, 29, 34,
 53, 58, 159, 166, 185

*Ezekiel*, 10, 15, 16, 29, 33,
 46, 48, 56, 130, 134, 138,
 157, 166

# F

*First Apocalypse of James*,
 16, 100
Five Adams, 146, 147

# G

Gabriel, Archangel, 46, 140,
 142, 163, 164, 167, 197
Gaia Hypothesis, 44, 169
Geburah, 126, 136, 137,
 142, 155, 172, 174, 177,
 193
Gehinnom, 180
*Genesis*, 14, 22, 24, 28, 47,
 48, 53, 102, 140, 145,
 147, 148, 153, 157, 158,
 166, 173, 175
*Get Ha-Shemot*, 18, 208
Gilgamesh, 14, 79
Gilgul, 180
Gnosticism, 44, 94, 95, 96,
 99, 101, 104, 106, 119,
 122, 183
God, 10, 11, 26, 27, 31, 33,
 34, 35, 42, 44, 45, 46, 47,
 48, 49, 52, 55, 56, 57, 59,
 60, 61, 62, 63, 64, 71, 73,
 80, 96, 100, 103, 106,
 107, 109, 112, 113, 119,
 123, 128, 130, 132, 139,
 140, 144, 147, 148, 149,
 151, 152, 155, 157, 159,
 161, 163, 164, 165, 166,
 168, 173, 175, 180, 181,
 187, 190, 192, 197, 198,
 200, 201
Godfrey of Admont, 113
*Goetia*, 18, 197

# U

# V

# W

nformation can be obtained
Gtesting.com
USA
'200818
'90002B/59/P